NEW CONTEXTS: 3

First published in paperback and ebook
format by **Coverstory** *books*, 2022

ISBN 9781739766023 (paperback)

www.coverstorybooks.com

NEW CONTEXTS: 3

Coverstory books

Table of Contents

Foreword

Back in 2020, when the idea for *New Contexts* was first born, who would have thought that two years later we would be onto our third volume?

Achieving such a milestone seems proof enough that creative writing - in this case, poetry and short prose - is in rude health. It is also a tribute to our authors who continue to contribute a wide range of pieces in various styles and with the broadest of subject matter.

As previously, from the material submitted I have tried to pull together as representative a sample as possible, and whilst not every piece will be to everyone's taste, hopefully there is enough in this eclectic mix to stimulate and entertain.

Ian Gouge, March 2022.

Prospecting for Hope

Your caged stone heart drops
from the winding house
on a ticking windlass,
down shaft & shaft
as you seek hope.

                Lifting your lamp,
your feet blind,
you limp between pit-props,
choke in dust that glitters, mocks
diamonds in a feeble beam.

You search rock-fall
at the longest ladder's foot,
below stripped ranges, hills
where shadows ink the ground,
where veils of pitch fall long -

              light hard to reach -
and I follow: heft
spade or shovel,
blade or pick:
go mine the coal of hope

in the cast
& shaft of darkness:
to hold warm,
fast,
in my cold hand.

                                  Lizzie Ballagher

The Train

I'd driven this road a thousand times
okay maybe one hundred
alright honestly at least fifty
after all I was 18 or so but to be fair
I'd ridden this way with Mom
before I learned to drive
before I was permitted to drive on my own.

So what were the odds that my teenage brain
diverted by radio, familiarity
and thoughts of at least one boyfriend
what were the odds that I
the only car on the road
would see, would even notice
the railroad lights flashing?

No crossing gate existed
to stop the traffic
to save a life
just an over-the-road high above
the tracks set of lights
subtly announcing their bulletin -
a forthcoming train.

And then, what were the odds that I
stopped a safe distance as I had been taught
sitting with the radio, the familiar
the thoughts of the boyfriend(s)
that I would notice the car
pulling next to me, pulling past me
then stopping squarely, solidly
in the middle of the tracks?

What were the odds that I
witnessing this and repeatedly
honking the horn, would see
that the car remained on the tracks

unmoving, horrifying
and I, climbing out of my car
would run waving and shouting

then watching as the train
slammed into the car, never
slowing its locomotion as it came round
the bend in its circuit, and I
leaving my car idling and unattended
would run headlong through the brush
along side of the tracks

for the train had finally come to a stop.

Clare Bercot Zwerling

The Untitled
for Graeme Edge

I am not itself anymore
not as light as I'll ever be
but lighter than I've ever been
I am not   not

Discarded wisps of down adorn
my thinning twigs so
long ago wove and
finely flotsam padded

I   a ghost of tenderly brutish moments
anon to be tossed by shapeless
hands of wind and rain
rock-a-byed to the cradling earth

or flung again to the freedom of air
oh that one last at last longed
for flight   unmanned spirit cum
quickening I   isn't life strange

Clare Bercot Zwerling

Marriage Certificate, Belfast 1914

Under 'Occupation' he's described as *Rifleman* -
same regiment as his father. She's a *Seamstress*, a gentle
way to earn a living until you hear the clatter of fifty
treadles clanking at the shirt factory on Queen Street.

She learns how to stitch a straight French seam,
fit a perfect sleeve, bind a buttonhole - enough skills
to make a wedding dress. Later she'll fashion
a Christening gown from the skirt.

I see her open her sewing kit, take out scissors
to unpick tight stitches around the waist. I hear
the rap at the door, an awkward boy standing,
cap in hand as her world falls to pieces, a single
white thread still hanging from the needle.

Margaret Beston

Last Dance of New Fire

My final day, we drive from Mexico City,
climb the peak of Cerro de la Estrella,
where your ancestors performed a sacred
ritual to bring back light to the world.

We picture a midnight procession of Aztec
priests robed in the insignia of gods.
They wait beneath a dome of stars
for the Pleiades to reach its zenith.

We picture the terror of the people, no light
but the light of stars - all flames, possessions,
destroyed to placate the Sun god. They cower
in shadows, fear the end of the world.

And then - first sparks - torches lit from fire
fuelled by a human heart, new flames carried
to every temple, every home. There is joy,
rejoicing: the sun will rise again.

Skyscrapers slice heavy evening air,
city lights pierce an indigo sky
as hand-in-hand we make our descent.
The moon is rising, we have lost the sun.

Margaret Beston

*Every 52 years Aztecs believed the world would end unless all fire and possessions were
destroyed. At a Ceremony (Dance), a New Fire was started in the chest cavity of a human
sacrifice.*

Bastide (Tournon-d'Agenais)

The valley shimmers beyond shuttered windows.
In the citadel, the streets sleep away centuries,
late sun snaking through their cracks,
its old pathways sure as the goat-tracks on the hill.

A black cat curls on a car's bonnet,
another luxuriates in the gutter,
a third is liquid sunlight under a doorway,
it pours and dissolves between geranium pots.

At the corner, the rhythms change:
a shaded bench melts into three figures,
a trio of women plumply ensconced
in the ripened hour, habituées of the lane's siesta.

Chatter rises and falls with the swallows,
the hands describe, circle, shake the air,
laughter crackles and transmutes
in their easy traffic; the minutes cling to them.

Now a lean grey feline leaps into being,
whiskers trembling with significance.
A shadow shakes itself into dog, raises its head.
Something is occurring in the invisible.

The black cat rolls over, spills off the car, is gone.
One of the women rises, sashays her story,
opens her front door, teases, cajoles.
The dog follows with his eyes, his snout; alert.

What is it that shuffles along the edges,
that slips through stone arches and rusted gates?
The day sags and is replete; evening hovers.
Who is it that passes this way?

Zanna Beswick

The Laying Out

Laying out the body
is something I've not understood before:
macabre but necessary; an embalmment.
The body itself is in repose
fixing structurally a final time
stretching out the limbs
crossing the hands, or not,
letting any last remains
of oxygen or methane become
part of the outer world again:
the integrity of chemistries.

But laying out the body
is a washing down of forages
the news from elsewhere,
a loving and smoothing:
the final soothing of flesh.
The intimate nooks, exquisite
curls of hair, the skin of
lime, plaster, bone, stone,
the gaps or the missing steps
of a life cleansed here
with a first and last scent of leaving.

Blemishes, freckles, bruises
the crannies of stories the chest wall holds,
where nails hang, or are as perfect
as at their conception,
the ridges of the roof of the mouth
revealed - are all delicately
hidden again, the lives and ledges
caressed just once more.
Soon the spiders, mites, the unknown,
will enter the crevices, make their
path through, love in a different language.

But for now the window-eyes are closed
gently, shuttered from sun or starlight.
The sounds of the living depart.
There is no way to say goodbye
that holds you to me but this:
this washing, this filling, this brushing;
letting your place become as silk
its memories a fabric
of vegetable colours, textures, rich soil.
Tenderly I slip the key into its hole

and lock the door for the last time.

Zanna Beswick

Skin Hunger

Fossilised footprints hold their story
beside pockmarks of ancient rain,
left by people who lived lightly, left
only a few bones, empty shells, and a record
of holding hands told in the disposition of steps.

I link arms with my mother, who shrugs
me off - *I can manage* - tuts at the easy entwining
of the young but sighs *I wish your father had been
more demonstrative*, and clutches me as last words
fail.

A finger wombwarm curls round mine
sure as bird to branch - grows to rock
his own child on the edge of sleep; passes
from hand to hand, safe, smelling of tribe,
forbidden now: don't touch. Must touch.

After sixty years we two still lie together
in a habit of closeness; your familiar body
curved around my back cherished
beyond fleshlife, fossilised into more
than ourselves.

Christina Buckton

Virus

the most vulnerable went first -
embrace cuddle fondle
stroke
hold -

then
whole swathes of past tense
sinking stinking like dead goldfish -
going going gone
remember when we once used to -

followed by the future - fizzing like a blown fuse -
next week shall we
expect hope plan intend -
let's meet -

words that mentioned
shaking hands and kissing
fell out
of etiquette books

memoirs were superspreaders -
descriptions of dancing the ceilidh
entwined in others' hot bodies
had to be censored

children stumbled over hug
in their reading books
open up got lost
in *lock down*

A handful of words
seemed to throw off the virus -
poetry
music
love -

they seemed to be flattening the curve
if you could remember what they meant

sometimes it was as if words were waiting for dawn
to sit up and say themselves

Christina Buckton

Solitude and Silence

I knew every rock in the fell. Every thistle. Every blade of heather. I knew each purple blossom. Each wine-hued blade of sheep's sorrel. How it danced in the wind. How it bent, sagging to the ground while weighed down with morning dew. I knew it all. Every inch. Every detail.

So when she showed up, no footprints in the frost to mark where she had come from, my initial thought was that she was not actually there. This woman who was staring at me blankly. My first thought was that I was dreaming. My second, that I had gone insane.

Perhaps those bilberries I had eaten hours ago had gone off, fermented or spoiled to alter the way I see the world. But when she smiled I knew I wasn't dreaming. I knew I wasn't insane. The bilberries may have been spoiled, but this woman was here before me. No such smile could be conjured up, be it by dream or psychosis. It was too perfect. Too warm. And yet, although a mere smile, a simple gesture, it wasn't without an unworldly charm.

'How did you get here?' Each word carried white mist, every syllable a spectral wisp in the cold air.

She did not answer.

'Who are you?' I ventured. And now her silence stretched to something beyond awkward. Strange and eerie. Stranger still, how she continued to smile. Strangest of all, how that smile seemed so familiar.

She was underdressed. Not for the occasion; no occasion in standing mute within a field. But she was underdressed. For the weather. Her summer dress, bare arms and uncovered head, her ankles, without stockings, exposed to the chill. Her shoes were wet, damp from brushing the dew-sodden weeds. Even while in my dry boots and wool sweater, felt cap over my ears, even then I felt the bite of the wind.

The nearest neighbor was miles away. My home, just over the hill.

'Let's get you inside,' I suggested. 'To a warm fire and a hot cup of tea.'

Still no answer. Maybe she'd prefer coffee.

As I opened the door to my home I became giddy. I didn't see many people. Tending sheep, overseeing the land. When I inherited the family plot I inherited the loneliness that came with it. Solitude and silence. And while this woman now entering my home didn't speak aloud a single word, somehow the silence felt broken. Her presence alone filled the empty air with music and song.

'Come,' I urged. 'By the fire.' This time of year the embers hardly ever dimmed to gray. The furnace was kept alive round the clock. Sometimes I felt as though the fire was the most lively thing in all of the fell. Its warmth was often the only comfort on offer.

I gestured to my favorite chair. I invited her to sit upon its soft, well-worn cushions. When she took a seat the rocking chair didn't budge a single inch. Its familiar creak, its tortured groan of strained wood, the echo of screeching floorboards under its pendulum sway, all the accustomed sounds that came with the comforts of the best seat in the house. All of them absent. Non-existent.

I added wood to the fire. I stoked the flame. An orange glow came to life and bathed her wet shoes in amber. I knelt and gently reached out. 'Take those off,' I advised. 'We'll dry them out by the fire.'

Words unspoken, her smile as bright and warm as the furnace aglow at my back, her expression conveyed that she had allowed me to remove her footwear. Those sodden, cotton shoes. So petite, I slipped them off and lay them gently upon the bricks as if they had been made of crystal. When I took her other shoe I thought of Cinderella. Her glass slipper. And what would that make me? The prince?

Now I was smiling too. 'I'll get you some tea.' I turned midway to the kitchen. 'Or would you prefer coffee?' But somehow I knew that she wouldn't. Somehow I knew it was tea. Always tea. In any case, she didn't announce her preference. She only smiled in silence.

I came back to her and to the warmth of the fire. The warmth of her spirit. I approached slowly, a hot black coffee in one hand, hot black tea in the other. His and hers.

'Here,' I set the mug on the table beside the chair, its wooden surface a network of rings from countless shared drinks, countless shared conversation and shared laughter. So many circles marring the wood, so many halos. Halos, like those on angels. Departed souls.

We sat in silence for a time. Once or twice I asked a question, offered a comment. 'How is your tea?' 'Your shoes will almost be dry.' My words were not ignored, but unanswered. And somehow that smile was enough to serve. No words were needed. So we let the quiet fill the room while we enjoyed our hot beverages.

I excused myself for a refill, asked if she would like the same. Without reply, I guessed that she was still working on her tea. I'd bring hot water so she could serve herself without my meddling questions, my irksome words. I made myself another round and returned to the fire.

My favorite chair was empty. My guest had departed. The silence remained.

Her shoes still lay set out by the fire. The same place that they always lay. Since the day that she died those years go. When the weather had turned and she never made it home. It was almost summer but that is never a guarantee. The first harsh lesson of living on the fell.

The weather turned. Her ankle turned. I had been drinking that evening. Drunk, I had turned in for the night.

I turned my wedding ring. A habit I've developed. Something I do to fill the vacancy of all that nothing. I cleared away her tea. Undrunk, it had gone cold.

I knew every rock in the fell. Every thistle. Every blade of heather. I knew each purple blossom. Each wine-hued blade of sheep's sorrel. I knew it all. Every inch. Every detail.

And now I remembered it all. All the details of those memories once lost. Blocked off by some phenomenon of self preservation. Severed from recall. It all came back. Every smile and every cup of tea. The warmth of my past. And now, the chill of the new day. Somehow, remembering it all, a life loud with laughter and filled with joy...

It made it all the more apparent upon the fell. Solitude and silence.

James Callan

New Beginnings

I consider the world as made for me, not me for the world. It is my maxim therefore to enjoy it while I can, and let futurity shift for itself. Tobias Smollett [1721-1771]

The storm had broken almost two hours ago. She was crossing Saddleworth Moor at the time, but that place was no more inviting in the summer. Shortly after, the Sat/Nav had packed up, forcing her to take a dozen or more wrong turnings. So ... not only was she late, but lost as well.

Living in Sheffield and travelling to Goole every day was a decision she was beginning to regret changing; but the new job in a small town on the Welsh border had sounded very tempting.

Another fierce blast of rain hit the screen, reducing visibility yet further. As the wipers managed to cope with the deluge, a sheet of lightning lit up the surrounding countryside.

Despite the torrential conditions, Kara thought she spotted a light over to her left. In that split second the road veered right but the car didn't. Instead, she wrenched the steering wheel, the rear tyres lost traction and the whole thing slewed across the road, through a narrow gateway, where it continued to slide for about another twenty yards.

Kara suddenly realized that her fate was in the lap of the Gods because she had lost all control.

The car finished up almost in the direction she had come from. The engine died. The wipers stopped, the lights dimmed, and a loud peel of thunder vibrated the little metal overcoat.

"Brilliant," she muttered.

Having seen enough films to know better, figuring it wouldn't re-start, she tried anyway.

Only when she'd accepted her situation did she jump out of the car.

Kara covered her head with a pile of manuscripts, realising that there was at least one advantage to being a librarian.

She lifted the tailgate: a quick rummage revealed an umbrella. As she turned, another sheet of lightning lit up a large gothic mansion that was all gable ends and turrets and pointed arches: not in the least bit alluring.

But the lights within one or two of the windows were, and so was the smoke from the chimney.

Dashing to the deep recessed porch she searched around for a bell but saw only a door-knocker in the shape of a wolf's head, reminding her of *An American Werewolf in London*. Three loud raps echoed cavernously throughout the building, which did little to alleviate her fear.

Kara suddenly thought of the writer's club back at Goole, in particular one twisted individual who had managed to kill someone in nearly every story. It was precisely the sort of situation he would put her in. He'd even managed to write off some poor woman with a body wipe.

She heard footsteps; the door silently opened. A wizened old prune, dressed in a black suit with a white shirt and black tie, stared out through the gap. Kara doubted he'd even seen a car, let alone know how to fix one.

She explained her predicament to him but she suspected he understood very little.

He replied in a language she didn't speak - which sounded like a hale of machine gun fire - before lifting his candle and beckoning her to follow.

She was unsure, but he had a pretty severe stoop. She couldn't see him giving her too much trouble. She supposed she could always go back outside, face what was coming, but that would be very little due to a lack of signal on the mobile.

The old man led her to the most enormous room. It was wall-to-wall, floor-to-ceiling books. A roaring fire burned in the grate, surrounded by fresh, dry logs. In the middle stood a mahogany writing desk, littered with more books.

She glanced around eagerly for a computer but was not saddened by the lack of one. It was only to be expected. There were two comfortable wing-back chairs close to the fire, with a small table in between.

The door closed. The old man - who resembled a butler - had gone.

She took a seat, but almost as soon as he had gone the butler returned with tea and cakes, lots of them. Now he was talking Kara's language.

He placed something on the arm of the chair but she was too interested in the pastries to notice what it was.

When he left she noticed a small footstool so she made herself at home, pouring tea and checking out the buns. She reckoned they must be locally baked because she didn't recognize any of them.

Kara then studied a portrait above the fireplace, wondering who it was. She stood up to obtain a closer view but there was no name to indicate the person's identity, nor for that matter was there an artist's signature.

He was pretty hot though, she could put up with a night in the mansion if all she had for company was him: he had fine features, a thick head of glossy black hair, a slim, toned figure; he was wearing the most exquisite suit.

She threw more logs on the fire and sat back in the seat, confident that the butler would return at some point with more information.

An hour passed and she was feeling quite sleepy. The old man had not made an appearance.

Kara glanced at the books on the desk, choosing one that covered local folklore.

She leafed through a few of the pages, where she came across a photo of one of the cakes she had recently eaten.

That reminded her, she wouldn't mind another, with possibly a round of fresh tea.

Kara went in search of the old man but he was nowhere to be seen. The kitchen - when she finally found it - was warm. It took her a while to locate everything. She made fresh tea. When she returned to the library she threw more logs on the fire, poured a cup of tea, grabbed another slice of heaven and decided to study the book.

Suddenly noticing the cake she had eaten in the book, Kara was interested in what it had to say.

Apparently, it was something called bannock: used as part of an ancient druidic custom allegedly performed at the celebration of Beltane, which involved distributing portions to all those present. One piece of the cake was blackened; the person who received the burned morsel was marked for sacrifice to the Gods.

Kara didn't like the sound of that. She was about to put the book down when she realized that all the buns she'd eaten were anything but black. They were fresh, and the first one had tasted very strongly of fresh almonds.

Reading on, she came across a paragraph about that. It said something about seeing your true love in a vision if that was the piece you had picked out first.

Kara yawned and sat back, too tired to study the legends.

❋

It was the morning sunlight streaming through the curtains that woke her. She was draped across the armchair, the fire had died but the room was still warm.

Suddenly realizing where she was she jumped upwards. The book fell on the floor.

She gathered her senses, put the book back on the desk and wandered through the house.

As with the night before, there was no one to be seen, not even the old man.

Out on the drive she was startled to see an RAC van in front of her car. The bonnet was up with the driver's door open. She noticed the mechanic as the engine fired into life.

Kara inquired as to how he'd found her. He explained something about an automatic tracker alert on the car, which sent out a signal to the breakdown centre.

If only the phone had employed the same technology.

Kara was eternally grateful if yet still mystified about everything.

After she had determined the mechanic was local, Kara asked about the house, explaining that she had stayed last night, sheltering from the storm. She also told him about the old man.

The mechanic's expression was strange.

"But no one's lived here for years. According to local tradition it used to belong to *Y Dyn Hysbys*, The Wise Man, or wizard. They say he learned about medicine and black magic from books, allowing him to see into the future, particularly on Halloween Night. Apparently, he gave out charms to ward off evil."

Kara was pretty spooked as she thought of the wolf's head pendant he had placed on her armchair, the one she was wearing around her neck but could not remember putting on.

The mechanic went on to say that among the powers of the *dyn hysbys* is the ability to know and reveal the unknown, especially events in the future pertaining to love and death.

Such powers might also be applied to commonplaces, like finding money that has been lost, or helping a Welshman to escape from an English gaol.

He was said to possess the power of breaking spells by undoing the evil perpetrated by witches and others. A *dyn hysbys* might also undertake to heal an animal or human by using charms and incantations.

The mechanic stopped there because he said he didn't like Kara's expression. He tried to soothe her nerves by adding that it was mostly folklore.

Regardless of what it was, Kara took once last glance at the house, and despite feeling bad because of the hospitality she had been shown, jumped in the car and set off to find the library.

Following the directions from the mechanic it took little less than an hour.

The building was very old fashioned and had been built using blocks and bricks similar to Yorkshire stone. Creeping Ivy adorned the walls, decorated with small hanging baskets and window boxes.

The caretaker met her and said that she was early and late at the same time, if that made any sense, but she knew enough about caretakers to realize they had a language of their own.

She was shown through to the head librarian's study and informed that he would be there in a few minutes.

After the caretaker left she turned and studied her surroundings, immediately hit by a sense of déjà vu. The room was a replica of the one in which she had been shown into the previous evening: with a log fire, a desk, two armchairs and the table.

She stared at the pile of books, trying to remember some of the legends she had read about, but could only bring to mind the one about the cake and seeing her true love in a vision.

Kara was about to turn to study the portrait when the door opened; in walked the head librarian.

Her heart missed a beat as she came face to face with the man from the portrait.

Ray Clark

Disemployed

A man is watching a pale sun on the rise
as it washes slowly across acres of mudflats
picking out shards of bottle-glass among the oar weed.
Grey birds dredge sludge with silent plodding and dipping.
Feeble sun and mist rise together.

This place has no memories or meaning for the man.
Like flotsam in the scum beyond the reeds
he is washed up on the edges of a town that will never be home.

As colour begins to seep back and
the ribs of boat wrecks creak in the tepid haze,
he ambles along a path of broken shells.
The reek of rot catches in his throat.
Left and right is salt marsh with spiky grasses,
ahead the silhouettes of abandoned gantry cranes
looming over brash new galleries and tapas bars.

Dawn like a dusk never to clear all day.
He opens a gate no longer fixed to wall or fence.
The path meanders among oily pools and silted ruins.
He follows it because it is there.

Nigel Ferrier Collins

25

The Gap

There is a gap between the cushions of the sofa
where small toys hide from the mouths of children.
Plunging hands risk cuts among the stickiness.
Despite this, whether lolling, bouncing, or snoozing,
sooner or later one is drawn to explore the soft recesses.

There is a gap behind the crazed mirror on the mantelpiece
where dockets are tucked. Here invitations,
appointments, and unreadable to-do lists
curl and fox.

There is a gap between house and garden
where weeds have been allowed to propagate,
providing food and shelter
for secretive slitherers and blood-suckers
that creep into your waking dreams.

There is a gap between bookcase and wall
where we hide what we wish we did not own
among things we are glad to own,
but whose attraction we are unwilling to explain.

There is a gap between what might have been
and our version of how it went, in which
we battle upstream for the source,
but are mainly drifting down to the chaos of the sea.

Nigel Ferrier Collins

On The Train

...I didn't realise you could reverse them...did you have a moment of euphoria?..what, the square one?..hello did you get my Email?..no I'm very happy she is doing two days...no we'll get her over on a visa and take it from there...not that Tuesday the other one...I said "dodging", what is your mind like!..very late for everything actually...I'm a very happy man...it can't fail its MOT on that, it means the freeing of slaves...is who with me? I don't think I know a Frances...don't bother with the wine we've just taken delivery...fourteen...yes, really, fourteen... he's David's, not Tony's...don't sell anything until after the meeting...that's very interesting, I think...Haywards Heath where the train will divide...there is a toilet but it's locked...let's do that again only without you know who...not tax deductible...nor that...probably blocked...well it's said now...I'm a very happy man now its settled...sorry you're breaking up...missing budgie!..beige!..the London office is twenty-four-seven now...Wicked...the show...the musical...text me that joke about the government...all it means is that it never really gets cleaned...I'll use it when I go to Madrid...I'm a really happy man now we've slotted her into place...have you looked behind the cabinet?..what about the cat basket?..the conference won't start without me...sleep is what you need mate...Romanian actually...year seven are eleven oblique twelve...it doesn't mean that kind of discipline...turtle necks? Of course I remember!..you can't lose something you never had...no, its called missing...well tell her the truth...she is a solicitor...I'm a very happy man...it's like saying the UK has gone to the dogs; from what?...you're echoing...I don't think I'm who you think I am...that's OK, it happens...ear-plugs going in now and weird film starting...and you...vote what?..who are they?..sleep mate, just think sleep...you don't need a dog to walk...stroll...well, yes strut if you must...seventeen point five million...pounds not dongs...consultant could mean anything...everybody is younger than you...lamb...it's a cut of lamb, always has been...very very happy...mother is still mother and showing no sign of...she is home...you're watching the third series...trust me you've skipped the second series...if you look like you did the last time we met I would avoid video conferencing...cineraria...don't make me spell it...well, if you haven't noticed it may not matter...there are no contingencies in an emergency, its all contingency...

Nigel Ferrier Collins

Silk

The silk on my bra strap is torn,
gossamer stitches strain apart
and expose an everyday elastic band
that has supported me
from the shoulders all these years.

29% Silk, 7% Elasticine. Made in China.
Expertly engineered by Eastern women,
heads bent over machines, chatting
as they edge moulded padding
with rose-patterned lace.

My Western breasts are flattered
by their craft, held together by their clasps.
Only they see the under wires, tell their daughters,
heads bent over homework, of the sharp ends
they cover with soft fabric.

                                        Adele Cordner

The Drawer

I took it out of the drawer today. I keep it in there with all the other stuff I don't need. A lunch box in the shape of a cat's face, candles with wicks that won't light, and an array of panty liners in all different shapes and sizes - free samples off the internet. I have to tug the drawer hard so it opens. As if it's resisting my nostalgia. Rummaging - it's there at the bottom - an ashtray in the shape of a skeleton. Bony fingers on the edges to rest your cigarette. The ash built up when I used it. I'd get a cotton bud and pretend I was finding the remains of someone important. It was thoughtful of you. I was going through a phase at the time.

You were embarrassed when you gave it to me. I said thank you, even tried to hug you. You tensed up. Shoulders and arms stiffened like bookends. You'd never acted like that before we found out.

I can't bear to throw it away. It might come in handy if anyone needs a spare ashtray when they come over. Nobody ever does, they always want to share. Maybe I'll get it out one Halloween if I ever have a party or something.

I heard you were living on Eldridge Street, just past the pub and off the main road. I know it's one of those big four bedrooms with the massive back gardens.

I've thought about that for weeks. You said we'd have a house with three bedrooms. We'd have our bedroom and there'd be a games room for you and a makeshift library for me. Said we'd be happy, said you were happy. "We'll fill it with noise," you always used to say, "We'll keep the neighbours up all night, because we'll host all the parties, people will be over all the time." I wonder now how just two people could fill a house with noise all the time. Even if your nephews stayed over it would have only been now and again.

You're living next door to my friend's mum on Eldridge Street. Her mum's getting annoyed with the trampoline and finding footballs in her garden that she has to throw back over. I don't know why she told me. If it was the other way round I wouldn't have dared mention it to her.

Do you remember that day we went to the Circus? The first year we were together. I'd never been to the Circus before. I wouldn't go to one if it had animals in it. I thought it was cruel, you thought I was sweet. We found one that July and the stench of sawdust and sweat overwhelmed us and children ran around us as we waited in the queue. I wore a floaty dress with poppies on. You said I'd never looked more beautiful. I'm wearing it now, but it's got a little tear in it. One child knocked so hard into your back that you nearly ended up on the floor. "We'll teach ours to look where they're going" you laughed.

I wrote a letter to you one night. I licked the envelope, addressed it, even put a stamp on it. I was glad when I sealed it - so I couldn't be tempted to read it again. It was six pages long, front and back, I surprised myself. I don't know if I had any real intention of sending it. I wrote about our day at the Circus and the house we dreamed of and then I wrote about everything else too, I think I repeated myself here and there. It might have made a difference if I'd have sent it. There are times when I don't blame you, or me, or anything except that letter, as if it was the window of opportunity - missed. I burned it on New Year's Eve. I sat there whilst everyone was outside singing Auld Lang Syne and watched the edges of the paper curl into a ball.

Sometimes I wonder if she's got a drawer like mine. Little keepsakes that she takes out now and then. I bet her furniture isn't flat pack though so when she opens her drawer it comes out smoothly. And when she looks through she won't feel any pain because hers will be filled with good stuff like your son's tiny wristband from the hospital.

Charlotte Cosgrove

trimming the sails

i've given
up on perfection
having known
it i don't
expect lightning to strike twice
so though i never

say never
and love all shades of
blue it's not
the color
one wants one's skin to be so
i'm not holding my

breath waiting
for another prince
charming to
to show up
at my door with roses and
and a ring to sweep

me off to
a paradise that
probably
isn't one
but i wouldn't mind a smile
and a hand to hold

R C deWinter

Gladioli

'life will go on somehow; life always does'

You hear these words as you observe
the gladioli in the vase, buds opening
day by day, a blood-red ostentation
inexorably ascending the inflorescence,
and you think of such as Anne Boleyn,
Lady Jane Grey or Mary, Queen
of Scots - each cut off in their prime
by bright keen-edged steel blades.

Gladioli, named by Pliny for their leaves,
shaped like gladiators' swords - apt
to cleave flesh - growing green and tall
until the knife sharper than their leaves
cuts them through, brings them down,
to be bunched, stacked and packed,
exquisite corpses, cellophane wrapped,
sacrifices made to the gods of trade.

A small wasp, knowing nothing of this,
goes, flower to flower in necromancy,
feeding on sweetness, dusting itself
with grains of once-hopeful pollen;
it's like Anne, Lady Jane, or poor Mary,
the executioner's blade sealing their fate,
ending their connivance in intrigue,
lessons learned, but manifestly too late.

                                        Phillip Dunkerley

She speaks with a strange intonation, a peculiarly-located rise in her voice as if the person who taught her English had overlaid the rhythms and inflections of an entirely different language: French, or German, or Pig Latin. It also seems she has never acquainted herself with the full set of letters in the alphabet; some are intermittently missing, certain combinations utterly compromised. And occasionally, unsure she has got her meaning across, she replays whole phrases - most often with no alteration in the words she uses or their sequence - as if repetition is the guarantor of understanding.

"I 'ad chips for dinner, I did. Chips for dinner. Those wavy ones. The ones like waves. But if you cooks 'em for too long they gets crispy on the outside, and I don't like crispy chips. Not when I 'ave 'em for my dinner."

Her voice accosts him from over his shoulder. Sitting at the front of the tram, he places her perhaps four rows behind him, the tone of her voice slicing through the air between them as if it were no distance at all, as if she is almost in his ear, intruding. He wants to turn and look, to assign a physical form to the voice. Perhaps doing so will remove the threat.

"Me boyfriend, 'e likes chips an' all. But not those wavy ones. So I 'as to do two lots when he comes round for dinner, 'cos he don't like those wavy ones. Says they're a waste of space, whatever that means. They're just chips, ain't they? Chips for dinner."

It is a voice that defies age. He imagines it belongs to someone who is younger than himself; there is a lazy, slovenliness about it he can only attribute to youth. Yet there is also something else. It is not wisdom - how could it be?! - but an undercurrent which suggests not maturity but experience; experience in the sense of having lived for many years, nothing more. He roots the notion in the way she says 'boyfriend'. It is not spoken with the caution or flush of youth, but with a brashness suggestive of someone who, in spite of all other evidence, is cognisant they are crossing a boundary, stealing a word from another vocabulary, one to which they should not be party.

"Sausages 'e likes. Beef ones. It's 'ard to get beef sausages these days, ain't it? 'E don't like all those fancy sausages with fancy flavours, me boyfriend don't. Not with apple or onion or whatnot. 'E likes beef. And it's 'ard to get your 'ands on beef sausages, ain't it? Used to be easy. Used to be all there was when I was a girl, beef sausages. Got 'em from the butchers at the end of our road; the one wot ain't there any more.

Lovely sausages 'e 'ad, that butchers. Me boyfriend would 'ave loved those, 'e would."

It is an assertion which places her in time. She is older than she sounds, older than the language she uses. And he wants to turn around even more as a result. He finds himself guessing. She is probably older than thirty based on what she has just said, and he instinctively feels the need to bestow more years on her but is unable to do so without evidence.

"Yes."

It is another voice; a companion piece. And he wonders if the unbalanced exchange is one in which this second person has been innocently trapped; as if they simply took a spare seat on a tram and found themselves adopted. It is a 'yes' delivered by someone without choice. Hidden in that single word is an implicit desire for the tram to go faster - or for the voluble woman to get off at the next stop. It is a 'yes' that contains more of the 'no' in it; a 'yes' that is a plea for help, an unspoken desire to be rescued.

"I don't mind 'em, sausages. But I likes fish fingers better. 'Specially with wavy chips. But me boyfriend, 'e don't like fish fingers; so when 'e comes round for dinner I 'as to cook two lots of chips and sausages and fish fingers, 'cos if I didn't what would we eat, eh?"

Attempting to block her out, he tries to focus on the city centre as it subsides into inner suburbs: a terrace or two, the hint of a new development, tired offices, a park and a school beyond. The tram stops three more times, and even though he tries not to listen he is unable not to collect the words she insists on repeating. 'Boyfriend' accosts him like a slap round the face, as does 'shopping' when she makes a seamless segue from the subject of her dinner.

"I likes Asda, I do. Sometimes I goes to Morrison's 'cos there's one just round the corner too, but I likes Asda better. And B&M. That B&M's good for some things too. But not sausages. Asda's good for sausages. My boyfriend likes 'is sausages from Asda."

And even though the topics have varied a little, the way she relays them creates a blur, a noise lacking any distinction.

The 'ding' of the bell causes him to look up to where the 'Stopping' sign has been illuminated once more, and as the tram slows he realises he can no longer hear her. He is aware of the second voice saying 'Bye' as if he has time on replay, and cannot help but register the relief embodied in the word.

When the tram stops it is outside a small parade of shops. Ahead, he can see a supermarket - Morrison's - squeezed between two charity shops, a

Clinton's cards, a bookmakers. One shop's window is whitewashed and boasts a 'To Let' sign that hangs slightly askew. He waits.

A woman appears by his window, pauses before crossing towards the shops, and he knows it is her. He catches her in profile for a moment and is surprised. She is at least fifty, if not much older. She has a face worn down by living, the naïve juggling of the everyday. Cocooned in a too-familiar grey raincoat, she tugs a dilapidated shopping trolley behind her, its left wheel slightly out of alignment. Her walk is a shuffle; she stoops a little; her hair, grey and wispy, looks too thin to be controllable.

As she reaches the far pavement, the doors of the tram slide to a close, and he feels the soft jolt of motion. In safety now, he can turn his head to watch her, and just before she disappears from view he sees her accost a pedestrian who just happens to be heading her way, and he imagines a story about chips and sausages being re-told as if buried within it are the secrets of the universe.

Ian Gouge

Ballad of the Preacher, the Poet, and the Psycho

Modern society laments the lost words of poets of antiquity. Painstakingly hand-copied onto papyrus sheets, few and far between, many faded and disintegrated in accidental fire, apathetic neglect, and purposefully channeled moral hysteria.

Sappho's name, for instance, is prolific, particularly when measured against the floating scraps of lines and severed words, translations of translations, that survive to read in the present day. Some of us find it agonising. Many of us pretend to. At the very least it's curious, trying to squint through the murk and comprehend another place and another time: a time when it took sweat and backache to produce words, rather than just two thumbs sliding across an overheated screen, faceless, and filibustering from an imagined podium over the top of even more of the faceless in a digital glut of informational junk.

Hopefully the servers and satellites end up more frail than papyrus. When people study our world centuries and millennia in the future, hopefully the pixels will have long scattered, the hardware obsolete, crashed, and beyond repair. I find myself envious of the generations long before us, that were able to leave behind some mystique, some intrigue, before they disappeared from the face of the earth. Quality over quantity, always.

Imagine being an historian in the year 4053, scrolling down a mummified Twitter, an endless toilet wall, but without the mildly worrying curiosity of what would actually happen if you called that number scrawled above the toilet paper dispenser.

Gouged out words and fabricated jargon: vitriolic, moralistic, verbose but with neither style nor soul. You need at least one.

But I'm not an entirely unrealistic romanticist of the past. No matter what the time or place, human society usually has to be in some moral panic over something. If it isn't, then a black hole sucks us in and everyone dies. You wouldn't want to die would you? No, probably not. At the very least I know I'd get icy cold feet at the last minute and need to stick them back into the furnace of group outrage to stave off the frostbite.

What makes me think I'm any better?

Because I'm a good person, I'm a smart person. Therefore I felt compelled to slide my thumbs across this overheating screen to make this post.

Grown adults screaming and twittering obsessively into the electronic abyss from their virtual soapboxes. It was better at least when you had to go and procure an actual box that would take your weight, then carry it outside where you had to look at people's faces and let them look at yours.

I remember better times.

Do I remember better times? I'm not so much a nineties kid as opposed to born in the nineties. But still, that has to count for something, right?

Everyone thinks they remember better times.

Everyone thinks they're enlightened, an expert, pretending they didn't just start caring about *insert cause here* five minutes ago when the hashtag started trending.

The falling-out between Oscar Wilde and his frienemy James Whistler completely soaked the broadsheets with searing hot tea in the eighteen-eighties. Each would make two copies of a hate-letter to the other, going back and forth, sending one to the actual recipient and the second to the press. Readers would send in comments to be published alongside; either team Wilde or team Whistler.

Pretty much an analogue Facebook feud.

I guess it's kind of comforting to see; a basic aspect of human nature that's common no matter what era you happen to be living in. But analogue has limits. Eventually people have to get on with their day. And there was still something literary in the way Wilde and Whistler threw their public tantrums.

That, of course, was before Wilde got nuked by a monumental cancellation.

"We live in interesting times," they say.

Makes me cringe.

We live in cringey times.

Wait, I'm not the centre of the world? How dare you? You hurt my feelings, such violence. So now I'm going to hunt you down, knife you in the guts and rip out your intestines.

But not before I respond to that last client email...finish work at five...pick up my kid from preschool...

At least the manipulative radicalisers, the greedy dictators, the petty schoolyard bullies of last century could say it to your face. At the very least the worst of the worst could usually string a half-decent sentence together, something that meant something even if it was horrible.

Is that a terrible thing to say? Are my priorities really fucked? Am I talking shit from behind a screen, just like everyone else?

Probably.

I'm a product of my time.

And that's what scares me the most.

Katie-Rose Goto-Švić

Adultery

Hank jumped not hearing someone creep up behind him. Caught spying on his own wife, Hank didn't know why he felt guilty. She had been texting again, smiling looking down at her phone while he was outside trying to get a handle on his lawn.

The baby had cried. He looked in the window. His wife held onto that phone like she had held onto that baby fat. Not that it bothered him, the baby fat at least. The crying did. She eventually, not as quickly as he had wanted, bent down to pick up the baby seeing the full head of black hair.

"I'm sorry." He said turning around to see Charlene, his neighbor, staring at him.

"I said, the lawn's really coming together." She smiled holding onto the leash of a small French Bull dog which Hank considered wouldn't run away if the apocalypse were bearing down on him.

"Well, that's the thing about weeds." Hank smiled trying not to look at her cleavage, "If you don't pull them out by the root, they come back."

His mind drifted back to that baby head of black hair. The only person he knew with black hair was the guy across the street two doors up. Hank naturally looked up to the house as Charlene asked another question he didn't hear. The man with black hair happened to be leaving his house and getting into his Mercedes.

"Yup," Hank tried, nodding, "Slowly but surely, the lawn's coming together."

Charlene laughed.

"What?"

"I asked how your wife and new baby are doing?"

"Fine." Hank said watching the Mercedes back out of his driveway and honk as he drove past them.

"Nice car." Hank said not sure what else he could say.

"It's not as nice as you would think on the inside. He couldn't get all the extras."

"How do you know that?" Hank asked.

"I went for a little spin." Charlene said with a little smile. "Don't look so shocked." "Sometimes you have to have a little fun."

Hank wanted to protest that she was married. He was married. The man with the black hair was married. She turned and left. He stared a beat too long before catching himself.

"Howdy Neighbor." Another neighbor with a dog. This one lived three houses up.

"Hey! How are you doing?"

"I didn't know woman that age could look like that. Otherwise, I'd turn mine in for a remodel!"

Hank didn't know how to respond without a weak smile. Charlene was the only neighbor whose name he knew. His eyes followed her going into her house across the street and closing the door.

"You're not?" His neighbor asked with a sly grin.

"Not what?"

"You and the lovely Charlene?"

"Hardly, I barely have enough energy to handle a newborn and postpartum wife, never mind anything else."

"Be careful. I hear she gets around."

The dog began walking down the sidewalk. The neighbor nodded as he started on again. Hank wondered how he had gone from a twenty-year-old never wanting to have a conversation about his lawn to not having friends anymore. There were work friends, neighbors, and family, but no real friends to talk to about things that rattled around your head like a penny in an empty coffee can. No one to confide your deepest thoughts in anymore, there was no one to share those unspoken suspicions.

*

It was the Mercedes man, Hank thought pulling up more weeds. His baby didn't even look like him even though everyone spoke the contrary. People were supposed to say the baby had the father's eyes and mother's ears. No one would say, doesn't look a thing like you. But inside he knew that dark hair destined to fall out and make the baby as bald as he was getting now couldn't undo the suspicions.

Paternity leave was a joke. He wasn't getting any pay. He just wanted the time with his new family. Lately, his wife seemed more like a roommate than anything else. Paternity leave ended and then quarantines were announced. Some people wore masks. Others didn't. He hummed a new take on an old Jimmy Buffet song, "Wasting away again in Corona-ville."

When Charlene's door opened, he turned to look. Certainly, she shouldn't be coming outside in her pajamas so late in the morning, but there she was. Almost angry at her indecency, he turned away.

"Hey Hank, how's the yard coming?" Charlene shouted from her yard before crossing the street.

Hank patted both hands against each other and stood up. "Just fine."

That was the thing with neighbors, you have to be nice. You don't want to start something that could end up being like the Montagues and Capulets. That part of the story was probably in a compendium of editor's notes talking about how they originally were just neighbors who one day Hank Montague didn't say hi to the busty Charlene Capulet.

"Uh, Hank...." She smiled

"Oh, I'm sorry." His mind trailed off as his eyes drifted across her pajamas.

"It's fine. How's those Gladiolas coming in?"

"Uh... Gardenias. They're looking good. I was worried that they might not do well, but they've been growing strong. I bought three to see how they did before I got more." Then frowning, "But still no blossoms."

"They're nice. Like a little family. Well, take care Hank."

The sun was getting hot. Maybe it was best to go inside. Cursing himself as he walked up his front steps, you would think he would have more self-control than a middle schooler, but that wasn't the case. Then a small smile to himself, most men had little self-control.

"They say women cheat because there is a loss of intimacy. Men cheat because there is an opportunity." A man's voice echoed through the kitchen.

"What is that sh...." He started and then looked at the baby.

"It's a sermon from Pat Arnold. I was trying to listen to it. I think we should be trying to go to church one of these days. You know," looking at the baby, his wife a gave a small shrug, "It might be good to just teach him right, you know. Not like we were taught."

"Like we were taught?" Hank said feeling out the words barely above a whisper. Had he really been raised so awfully? He hadn't been to church in a long time and maybe it would be good. He looked at his wife, his head slowly bobbing up and down. Had their wedding been the only time they've gone to church before? Had they talked about faith?

"You know, for the baby."

"Okay." He said pointing to the sermon being streamed on her phone. "I didn't even know you listened to him."

She shrugged, "I don't know. Just someone recommended it. I checked him out."

He went over to the baby. He kissed the baby's head looking at the black hair trying not to think about it. Trying not to draw conclusions where there might not be. Wasn't church a place to go to for forgiveness? Wasn't church a place for someone to try and no longer feel guilty?

✿

The next time Hank was in his yard, he couldn't help the fantasy of his neighbor. It wasn't anything specific. It was just the opportunity. It was the moment of her opening the door and waving her hand ushering him into....

He shook his head. Why was he thinking this? Do men go through their own version of postpartum? Bringing up his own needs to his wife just felt selfish but running for someone else to meet them was worse.

He knocked and waved on the window as his wife held the baby. She turned to look. The baby had been up a lot the night before. Breastfeeding meant that he was sleeping while she was doing the nightly duties. He had offered to get up, but she wanted to do it. The wave was a need to just connect with her and take him away from whatever weird temptation was seizing him.

She turned without waving back. Hank stared at the top of the baby's head. The black hair foreign to his gene pool. Black hair like the color of the Mercedes. He began pulling weeds in a frantic fury without using his gloves. He tossed them in a pile, already feeling his hands burn with small cuts. Black hair like the man who drove the Mercedes, it was black like his neighbor's heart.

"Howdy neighbor!" The neighbor with the dog said. "How's that baby of yours?"

"Good." Hank said automatically snapping out of his anger.

"Before you know it, he'll be up and running. You know the backyard needs some attention too! Or is it just the scenery is better here than back there?" Turning toward Charlene's house.

"Getting the front in order, then moving to the back." Hank said not sure why he felt the need to justify himself

As the dog began to pull on the leash, the neighbor began walking again, "Maybe wear those gloves of yours. Your hands will thank you."

"I don't like the neighbors." Hank whispered holding the baby bottle as the baby drank. Thunder crackled out the window. "I don't like the weather either."

The baby let out a large coo dropping the rubber nipple as Hank's wife leaned over him looking out the window, "Yard's looking better. Maybe it's time to attack the back."

"Is this a conspiracy?" he said without thinking. "I can't believe it!"

"Believe what?"

"I'm getting there!"

"I know." His wife said. "I was just saying you're spending more time outside talking to the neighbors each day. It might be a better escape them by working in the backyard too."

✿

The hospital required them to watch videos about postpartum and baby care before they were discharged. Symptoms of postpartum included paranoia, depression, overindulgent appetite to lack of appetite. His wife hadn't really showed signs of anything.

As Hank watched her leave the room without comment, the baby dozing happily in his arms, he wondered if he weren't showing the symptoms of postpartum more than she. Rain began to patter against the window and Hank felt himself sink a little into the couch. His eyes grew heavy and began to lower.

"Hank! You can't sleep and hold the baby! You'll drop him!" Another warning from one of those videos. "I guess I can't leave the baby with you for second!"

Grabbing the baby from his arms, she left the room. Hank looked out the window and saw Charlene come home. The rain already making her clothes see-through. He watched her as she walked almost giggling to the mailbox. Was her husband ever home?

Charlene as if sensing his gaze looked up and waved at him. He watched her move slowly toward her front door. She turned and looked back across the street. His heart trembled in his chest as she disappeared from the open and inviting door.

Kris Green

The Maths Teacher

July.

She's thirty-two,
stroking blustery strands, dazzled
by evening sun on the Solent.
A boom swings loose,
connects.

October.

He lives for his teaching.
We lurk, just out of range.

A few, unlucky, breaktime convicts
build an allotment next to the field.

Pretending to listen to his lectures
about frost protection and manure.

Watching his fingers steeple, flex,
dibbing the earth for broad beans.

December.

His face is cracked like limestone.
Children, I've a surprise for you!

A murmur of excitement ripples.
From his satchel, he produces

a gift of clementines and walnuts,
all inspected and portioned out.

A merry Christmas, one and all.

The bell rings for morning break.
We toss the gifts on desks, run outside.

He leans down, counts the perfect fruit
and each little shell, back into darkness.

January.

The month of
rededication
washing clean
a cold ritual
the arithmetic
of breathing.

Lucy Heuschen

tomorrow's dawn

bruised reeds quicken in a warm west wind
I watch the strands of cirrus clouds
drift eastwards to tomorrow's dawn
through a veil of windblown hair

I watch the strands of cirrus clouds
remnants of last summer's smouldered dream
through a veil of windblown hair
mares' tails waft through mackerel scales

remnants of last summer's smouldered dream
the lofty ship that carried sails too high
mares' tails waft through mackerel scales
fanning ashes where my phoenix lies

the lofty ship that carried sails too high
drifts eastwards to tomorrow's dawn
sails lowered   veil lifting in the breeze
bruised reeds quicken in a warm west wind

Diana Killi

Joan

Slow round the corner.
Tap those bumpy flagstones. Don't trip!
It's Joan, brown-brogued, tweed-skirted,
white wisps straying from a fair-isle tam.
I help her across the road, into the park.

- You're very kind. Do I know you dear?
- Yes Joan, I think you do.

With dogged steps she claims
her bench below the willow tree.
She sighs and sits and waits.
Blurred dots of wilted crocuses
and jaunty daffodils catch her eye.

Teenage sweethearts waltz through
greening grass
in a hormone-zested clinch.

Joan knows -
when that smell in the air
stirs the dance in her feet
the sun in her heart
the caress of a breast
and the lust in her loins.
 - she's Joan.

Pushchair wheels purr past,
The young mum swings along,
cautions two tots on bikes.

Joan knows -
the nuzzle of her babes
the fear in her guts
hot arms outstretched
for a shielding embrace,
in a welling of love.
- she's Joan.

A jogger breezes by.
Firm footsteps, flashy shoes
- Nice morning love!

Joan knows -
by the push of the turf
the strain in her calves
the swell of the lungs
and the swing through a stile,
it's the top of the hill.
- she's Joan.

An old dear trudges down the path.
Legs heavy, head down,
back bent over Zimmer frame.

Joan knows -
it's the aches in her joints
the veils on her eyes
the jumble in her head
the grief in her soul
and the smile on her face,
 - she's Joan.

Diana Killi

Rock and Beethoven

The make of car eludes me, but his music
I can still hear - Beethoven's Fifth, its heavy
cadences removing any need for talk. Beyond
the windows, a big northern sky, and hills stretching
to the border. He was not a man for small talk,
preferring plot and exhortation, the world of work,
the politics of the right. Better to keep silent, enjoy
the view and the way Beethoven, Spring sunshine
and the borderlands somehow coalesced. He was
a natural driver, sweeping past lines of heavy trucks
with a nonchalant flick of his narrow, hairy wrist.

Then, out of the blue, mid-afternoon,
we stopped suddenly, in the middle of nowhere.
Nothing to see other than the border road,
grey and dusty in the sun, and a craggy hill,
its sun-lit face of white stone pocked with
handholds. Booted, eyes aglint, he almost ran
to the cliff, its lower stretch strangely smooth,
almost shiny. He turned to me, with that
waspish smile, then insisted on a leg-up. Typical!
He was not a man to be denied and I dutifully cupped
his sheep-shat boot in my two hands, while he reached
up, only thinking of the bare rocks above our heads.

He climbed for, what, half an hour? I
stared into the distant hills and the future.
Later that afternoon, we resumed the drive,
winding through the tree-green valley of
the Tweed, its waters silvered in the Spring light,
both of us rapt in thought, albeit blighted perhaps
by the penance of the mundane day ahead:
the Glasgow meeting, the suits, the stifled, high-rise
views of city life, the cut and thrust of here-today,
gone-tomorrow politics. After a few hours of tedious
wrangling across the table (all things unresolved),
we drove back south, dark clouds heavy with threat -
no rock, just Beethoven, sonorous and ominous.

Richard Knott

Shell Museum

He had seashells over his eyes while
she lay back on a slab of rock, for
all the world like Jackie Onassis,
her shades as black as night, dressed
in black too, comforted by an Iberian
sun, although this is Somerset and the
month is October. I am busy in the
shell museum, washing away the mud
of the Bristol Channel as I've been told
to do, and trying not to think about cancer,
hospitals, the state of the world. She waves
across the bay, that arc of grey, smoothed
pebbles, pleased that I am still following
instructions: the age gap may be as broad
and wide as the Severn, but I know my place.

Before we go and as the sun succumbs to
cloud from the west, he sets up the family
selfie: five of us, wide smiles but grouped
tight and narrow, me at the back in others'
shadow. He has removed the shells now, so
the camera holds five smiling pairs of eyes, all
agleam, although the sun and morning have
now both gone, and all that's left is afternoon.

Richard Knott

Borderline
Khartoum

He has a face.
Burned umber or ebony.
Scratch of beard.
I think he's wearing a white top,
maybe a shirt.
He has one leg, I know that,
and at least one questing hand.

The bush somewhere in South Sudan.
Thorny acacia, tufts of fingergrass.
A click. The endless now.
Pupils dilate, blood pours to legs
so he can run.
No more.

A crumpled iron shack
in eastern Khartoum before dawn.
He's cooking kisra flatbread
in a pan drizzled with grease.
Takes it off the flame,
gives two pieces of bread
to the boy in the corner, eats one.
A bullet case falls from his pocket, bounces and rolls.
The mongrel outside snarls.

Is he saying something?
Arabic. Guttural.
I am pressed between him
and braids of cars
washing down this side street.
He hops closer.
Should I stop, give tattered dollars
or hurry out before that van?
I step out, I never see.

Richard Lister

P.R.

There's all types of pea, see?
It's hard to make the choice
between:
Petit Pois, Baby Sweet,
Marrowfat, Steamfresh,
Pigeon Peas, Chick Peas...

SHIT!

In all that mass of teeming green,
how does a pea stand out?

There's lots of options and the truth is
everybody wants to shine

gotta get moving,
gotta get out there
gotta be fresh

branding is the neon in your name
so ask yourself:

what kind of pea are you?

Lindy Newns

An Abraham and Isaac Redux

Every week my father brings me to the top of the hill
To be bound, rope tight on my wrists like lineage, dagger held
Against my throat for at least an hour or so

I've come to think of it as our father-son bonding time
He searches for divine signs, any sign, prays
In double negatives trying to trick God into an approval

I take this time to watch the clouds, adorn
Headphones, I know the divots on the stone slab well
And make myself cozy

At night I'm chored with sharpening knives
Until they whisper my name, father pinches
My bony shoulders disappointed, wishes
To never see me become a man

I try to tell him that I don't mind my spilt blood being used
As currency for his salvation
But he invokes louder, ignoring my death-bed pleas;
My attempts to form our own holy pact

I ask if we can go to the lake one day instead
So he binds me with fishing wire, brings a dusty case
Of Buffalo Springfield cassettes
Which he plays softy, smokes Churchill cigars
But tells me I'm too young to enjoy them

He, eventually, begins talking about his father too
Won't matter, he thinks, I'll be dead soon and my tongue
Will taste God's call
Before it regurgitates the knowledge that his father would never care
Enough to sacrifice him, no matter what the Lord demanded

One day I grow bored, feel mischievous, find a ram
And cut its horns off to lay upon my head
I dress the beast in filthy clothing, then throw my voice from nearby
foliage
"Father, you've prayed devoutly and here I am
God has finally provided"

My father cradles the ram
Says "My son, you've grown so strong, I knew God
Would intervene, I knew you'd make me prouder
Than all the stars in the sky"

When they leave together I remain tangled in the bush
A passing angel wanders by, sees me and laughs, reminds me
That God will only demand sacrifice
Of that which is considered precious

Dante Novario

Being a Bad Bisexual

So what if I fucked the entire town
And left no survivors

So what if I like my blood
Violet, my dick doubled
And my heart atom-split
Into dangerous little pieces

So what if I force-fed parts of myself
To those who could not love me
And sewed up their mouths to stop any form of regurgitation

So what if I keep insisting friendship is a synonym
For flirtation and I secretly screw the voodoo dolls
Of everyone who ever rejected me

So what if I dip my ravenous hands inside your body
And write my name on every wall
Claiming ownership to something I'll never fully appreciate

So what if I put the bad in forbade, the ho
In abhorrent, and the lust
In slut

So what if my body is a temple repeatedly defiled, the gods
Worshiped there never even seemed to notice
And enjoyed the many new congregants

So what if I was a double-agent
Self-employed, betrayed everyone's trust
And walked out of those flames alive
Alone

So what if I self-fulfilled everyone's filthy predictions
And accidentally made prophets of them all

So what if I casually summon demons
To possess you, to force your voice
To say that I'm the sexiest thing you never loved

So what if the world looks at me in disgust, I'll put a paper bag
Over its head and keep going
Just like I always do

So what if I'm so greedy I'll go down on the sun
Instead, when the clouds swell and rise I'll be there
To suck them dry, to blow the four winds back
And never be satisfied, never turn around
And give everyone the satisfaction
Of transforming into delicious salt

Dante Novario

Burning at both ends

the flames lick the wax
of my candles in the cake
and tear through
my brain to
my 17th birthday,
a night spent
staring at you through a screen,
the light of my soul flickering
towards extinction
because you
blew out my candles prematurely
and no one
stepped in to tell me that
adults dont do that
to children.

now everyone celebrates
the ring on your finger
as i fight to celebrate
the age you once were because
how do i explain that
my soul is now tied to someone
seven years older than me
who couldnt be committed to
signing a birthday card,
yet
sentenced me to
years of circular reasoning
stemming from all the times he
told me i seemed older than i was,
then left me for acting my age.

i let the wax cascade into the frosting.
i lost my appetite.

Alfie Ormsbee

Bare Beauty

My daughter kicks and taps
in nearby lesson while I,
      I probe
stripped branches outside
my wagon, their twining twigs
      and bulges,
and my angst
at the bare tangle

of Mother's mind
Alzheimer is wintering.
Her supple leaves gone aflame.
then brittle underfoot.

"Why is your tummy
      like a
            watermelon?"
Mother greets her niece.

"Your mother's sweet,"
my friend said long past.
I kept leafed my bulging hurt
      refusing betrayal
      secreting my shame
the baring of her barbs.

Now they're out.
Dirt pocks my car window
streaks   transparent hearts.
Shedding anger
         needful
         daily
as raking up
November leaf drop.

Carol L. Park

Meet the Dad

We waited for my girlfriend's father near doors marked, "No Entrance." My beautiful, slim lady wiggled her hips away from my hand as the huge doors moved. Perhaps she glimpsed her father making his way. I knew his acceptance of me was crucial to her. My foot jiggled.

Taiwanese men in suit jackets burst out. Maybe she didn't want her dad to see us touching. He knew about us, reportedly. What would he think about a boyfriend who had never left the states?

Of the many black-haired people streaming into the San Francisco Airport International Arrivals lobby, all wore masks. Only a few, and Caucasian like me, showed their mouths and noses. I had given in to wearing a thin white mask for the sake of my girlfriend. My glasses fogged and my ears burned from the loops. For Xiao Dan.

Seeing her in a mask had once brought my chuckles.

"Why are you laughing? It's no joke!" Her brows pinched like tweezers and she stared me down. "I told you I've been following the homemade videos posted from PRC. It's more deadly than SARS. It's probably already reached Taiwan. Our second in command knows Public Health, and so things are done right."

I'd pasted on a sober look, but the so-called deadly virus loomed from afar. Now at SFO, watching all those who had born the discomfort of a mask throughout a 13-hour flight made it more plausible. A torpedo through my casual self-assurance.

Hustling around a uniformed driver meeting clients, a thin man in a navy suit and a striped tie made his way. His mask projected out, larger and probably thicker than the thin, flattish rectangular ones Xiao Dan and I wore.

Xiao Dan pressed toward him. To my surprise, she hugged him.

My sweaty palm jutted out, robot-like. "Nice to meet you, Mr. Chang. I'm Mike."

"Call me IB," he said

"Really?" I glanced at Xiao. The Chinese people I knew, except my girlfriend, loved formality.

"It's his nickname, for Americans," Xiao said.

Crinkle lines rose near his eyes - a smile the mask did not eclipse. At night in bed, I'd imagined myself making all kinds of cultural gaffes. Maybe this wouldn't be so hard.

"Was anyone coughing near you?" Xiao's intense dark eyes beamed into her dad's.

"No." He lightly touched his mask. "It's good protection."

"You exited so fast! Weren't there precautions?" she asked.

"Just the usual. Businessmen from China were onboard and everyone was careful. The virus will certainly come. Probably already here."

"People don't understand." Dan's sharp elbow jabbed my hips.

Called out as the skeptic. I had laughed when seeing the video of Taiwanese officials wearing full haz-mat suiting meeting infected cruisers. I'd labelled Xiao as OCD when she wiped down her phone with sanitizing wipes, and wherever we sat.

We ambled onward, IB pushing his roll-aboard, wheels squeaking, towards the elevator leading to the garage. We joined those waiting outside the entrance.

"And Mother?" Xiao said. I was grateful she didn't lapse into her language of birth.

"She's fine. Just bored. She doesn't go shopping much. And she gave up playing Mahjong."

"So do you order food?" Xiao asked.

"Yes. Food apps are springing up. They text after they've left the food outside our door."

I shook my head. The excess of caution appeared so boring, so isolating.

IB turned my way. "What do you think will happen here?"

"Can't say. Americans are famously optimistic."

Was that a chuckle swallowed or just a loud gulp? The gleaming elevator doors slid open. Two people got in, and I stepped toward the opening.

Xiao clenched my arm, holding me back. The collegial looking girl inside beckoned us. The doors closed as a portly man within shook his head.

IB turned towards me. "A small enclosed space isn't good. We learned through SARS and Ebola."

"Like constant vigilance?" I asked. Xiao had worn a mask since childhood, whenever sick, to mitigate spreading.

"Yes, it's necessary."

I'd seen the gleaming thirty story towers, one after another, on YouTube videos, like San Francisco on steroids. Xiao Dan's home. A density so unlike where I'd learned to ride my first bike. She was the first non-white woman I'd dated. Her keen mind, sensitivity and tact drew me. Her thoughtful essays with unexpected wordings attracted my admiration.

"Did Mother send masks?" asked Xiao. He nodded. "How did she get them?"

"She keeps a supply, and on hearing the rumors, she stocked up."

Early on the Taiwanese government ordered specialists to prepare to manufacture masks in Taiwan. Vending machines stocked them. The identity card required for purchase prevented buying more than three daily.

We reached my Hyundai Avante, and Xiao Dan insisted her father sit up front with me, something I hadn't anticipated. I'd have to make conversation. He handed wipes out, first to me.

"So many hands on that walkway." He spoke through his mask.

I'd thought nothing of touching that black rim, but he was right. I followed his lead in leaving my mask on.

"Taiwan has penalties for not wearing a mask?"

"$1,000. It will save the country much medical expense."

"Wow!" I thought it Draconian, or, at the least, hyper-vigilant.

I quieted. Xiao Dan had initially held her disagreements inside, probably I should too.

"Xiao has taught me a lot." I glimpsed smile crinkles.

"And what do you do?" said IB.

I cringed, but Xiao Dan reached out a hand to my thigh. That helped me overcome my trepidation about what her dad, a successful businessman, would think of me, an English nerd, in the time of tech and biotech and the general rush to degrees linked to high-income earnings.

I explained my specialty, and IB replied, "You must be very intelligent. Literature contains a culture and its history. It's important to retain."

My fingers had clasping the wheel had turned white. I relaxed them.

I exited the garage and concentrated on good choices. First one, and then anther fork, between San Francisco or San Jose. I squeezed between vehicles to reach the south bound lane. Futures diverging with astonishing speed.

Carol L. Park

Downsizing on Freecycle in a Pandemic

I am now vintage. Like the coney fur coat. My pink is dusty. Like the shoes. The shoebox tells my story in black and white and a medium block heel. The taxidermy fox is out, with his milky eyes and dusty brush; he's seen too much. The wicker basket is beginning to unravel, but it's a better basket than the one I don't have, says the brisk man, backing off, before our breaths collide. He avoids touching the latch on the gate. I put a wicker basket width between us. Yesterday, another man stood on the step. He gave me flowers, before he took my mother's sewing machine away. Three sickly yellow leaves, peeled away, left a tight, green cabbage, the ornamental sort, at the heart of the bunch. I heard them patter on the path at my feet. Her precious black and gold slipped away, without a sound. No goodbyes. Beyond the garden gate, there's another life. His wife will love it, he says.

Janet Philo

How Some Things End

'You're leaving! That's great!'

My boss releases his grip
on my neck.
That sort of thing
was not up for discussion
then.

'I didn't mean...
I should rephrase...' he said.
It's the budget thing...
you understand.'

Inside a Hindu temple,
candle light casts
shadows on
flickering walls of rain,
moving with the
drumming of
the storm.
Our shoes float
down the street
with the last
thunderclap.

I left a friend
without a hug.
She can't do hugs.
They leave her cold.
But we both know
how the quiet
currents flow

and part of me
remains
on the beach
drifting.

Janet Philo

A Tale of the Familiar

I don't look at you. I only have eyes for the box - a cardboard tower, upended like a dislodged Jenga block. I'm checking out the arrows. I should, of course, have trusted you. This is what you do. You know the importance of keeping the arrows pointing upwards.

You're on familiar ground. You deliver dreams in cardboard boxes every single day. I'm the one, stepping outside my comfort zone. This box contains my lockdown summer. Febrile imaginings of hot, staycation summer evenings, securely wrapped and safely upright, delivered to my doorstep. If only I can get this one to grow, I'll own the scent of paradise, for a month or so, just as the sun goes down. It's not much to ask.

You're kind when I start the conversation somewhere in the middle - miss out the pleasantries.

"It's my honeysuckle," I smile at the box. I'm thinking out loud, not talking to you.

"I guess so." You forgive my rudeness and join in the game of supposition anyway.

It is okay for you to go now. Your job is done. You are in possession of an image of my feet, next to the box. No one will question your delivery skills. I notice my yellow flip-flops clashing with the terracotta porch tiles, and become intensely aware of my toenails. All, except the big one, have outgrown their polish. But surely my toe data is safe with you. You must have signed something when you took on the job. And you have kind eyes.

But where are they now - those eyes? Your attention has turned left.

"You're a bit early aren't you?" A proper question bridges the gap between us at last.

I'd been thinking I was late, far too late to see the honeysuckle flower this year. But you've abandoned horticulture - the talk has gone elsewhere.

"You're early for Halloween?" Your eyes twinkle, as a daft moment lights up a dull day.

Your attention is focused on a besom broom propped against the porch wall. It was a present from my husband; one of those 'Saw this and thought of you,' things, but I'm not about to share such marital intimacies with you.

"I like to be prepared," I answer as you turn to go.

You turn back with a cheeky grin, (you feel as if you're on safe ground with this now, I can tell).

"I bet you've got the cauldron bubbling back there, haven't you?"

"Actually we've got a coven Zoom in half an hour," I reply. This is true.

You're still playful, in your safe zone; a smile from deep inside lights up your work day face, as you close the white van door, singing along to Sweet Caroline on the radio.

A familiar soft meow is lost in the sound of gravel crunching under your departing tyres, and my calf tingles to the touch of Grey Malkin's upturned tail.

Janet Philo

Falling Snow

changes everything
its silent insistence

mesmerizes

kitten-soft touches
melt
on skin
on hair

each breath's
a plume
of smoke

flake
follows
flake

padding
brokenness

smoothing
inconsistences

shielding
each
sharp
stone

forgiving
the muddle
and rubble
of existence

for a few
short hours

each
crooked branch
each
troubled life

glitters

Jenna Plewes

Unreal city

In a penthouse garden
a hooded figure tends a hive
murmurs to his bees

In empty offices lights
flutter like trapped moths
dying houseplants
crawl across desks

Ring-a-ring-a-roses
London's falling down

ambulances howl like wolves
figures shrouded in plastic
bend over hospital beds
roll dead weights
peer through fogged visors
at beeping monitors

bodies float in a sea
of unknowing, each breath
sucked from flooded depths

doors are sealed with rainbows
light dies with a sound
like the beating of wings

bring out your dead
bring out your dead

Jenna Plewes

Murano Blues

You say you don't remember
our time in Venice.
When you left me, you left
our Murano horse as well,
which I still have to remind me.
I see it every morning on what
was once our window sill.

The sun illuminates its flawless
glass, which at its heart is blue
as jacaranda trees, then by degrees
becomes lighter, cooler, until finally,
at its edge, is clear and cold
as any arctic stream:
just as your love for me grew cold.

Stephen Poole

The Discretion of Objects

Faced with the possibility of change
into, say, an orange or a breadboard
most things prefer to stay the same,
not indulge, but instead, refrain.

The molecules might make it viable -
adventure, we might say, or passing clouds
and in the morning all would be altered
but that, it seems, would go against the grain.

A leaf might tremble, blush or fall
but will not be commanded to dissemble
for such would not be within ipseity
nor useful for presaging rain.

We glory, of course, in dapple,
as did Hopkins; but movement
in that which stays in place
would disturb all nature's reign.

The things, like trees, are shy -
they peep from under coverlets of silk
and hate to disturb, sir, at breakfast,
lunch, or at any site of pain.

Table, bedspread, modem, meme,
we joy in our propensity to remain
within our bounded circle,
a hallowed, anthemic refrain.

David Punter

Silver Hearts

we called them silver hearts
we used to see them running
racing   flowing
an undulant underworld
through and among the wreckage

we never saw them clearly
the silver glint   perhaps
a drop of red
though there was no forage
no carrion no sudden kill

we used to still see them
even after the anaesthetol
though they were never still
a solid flow of liquid
silver sheens uncounted

at what we would still call night
though there was no longer night
just a shuddering dusk
we imagined them
imageless   free

they roamed amid the fallen
cupolas of nameless theatres
the harbour's detritus
the refuse-stricken nightclubs
where once we'd danced

once we followed them
until wilder creatures
reared in the darkness
blank-eyed and trembling
and we retreated to our huts

once maybe our hearts
were silver we thought
but now they are exiled
flowing along a land
merciless and free

David Punter

Scandinavian Winter Solstice

i

Goddess Beiwe stirs, wakes her daughter,
Beiwe-Neia. They bless dead animals with prayer,

build a sky-sledge from reindeer bones.
Night thickens as the Goddesses roam

solstice-velvet skies, studded silver.
Summoning rebirth, Beiwe shivers,

and Beiwe-Neia casts her breath
over snow and ice. Banishing death

they wake shrubs and trees. The green
stubble of caribou food will soon be seen.

ii

But Goddesses cannot protect the downy birch
threatened by warmth and the growth

of invading trees. Birch parasols shelter
perma-frost, for now, but the helter-skelter

of change stacks up bodies of starving deer
as tundra disappears. Sami tribes fear

the desecration of herds and their life.
Goddesses vanish forever from sight.

Jenny Robb

The Master and his Emissary
For Iain McGilchrist, author of the book of that name

Tap the app on your fitbit,
Nibble the bait of each online hit
Sniff the chrism of the algorithm
From ten billion whirlwind waiters
Serving the servers of Big Data

Two hemispheres of the brain, the left and right -
The Emissary and its Master -
The left brain loves to be certain, was born with the need to be certain
Is a dab hand at denial, loves to sort and sift and file -
Likes choices that are binary, doesn't sit on the fence -
If the theory it doesn't fit it slams the mind's steel curtain shut
Shouting 'Show me the evidence!'

The right brain sees the bigger picture,
Tunes into meaning and deeper structure
Handles ambiguity and inner nature, the creature in us
It *empathises*, makes eye contact, tunes into the human,
Connects all the impulses so we're more than just neurons and atoms:
The quantum of Richard Dawkins' blind watchmaker in the machine.
To the right brain we're both wave and particle,
A glorious indefinite article that breathes the mystery
Of biology, the intuition of cosmology.
We can understand without needing to prove
How Keats' rainbow is more than its explanation,
How love dissected in the scalpel's exploration
Is just sacrilege on a slab in the path lab,
How even non-believers kneel at the altar of creation.

So we traded the heart's nation without even knowing
Fracked half the poetry in two, now we reap what we're sowing -
What's the left brain sucked us into?

WHERE DID ALL THIS HATE ORIGINATE?

I mean all these vultures learning to tweet,
Hyenas ripping rotten meat
Misogynists hunting in fake six-packs
Vendors of fear
Monetised pornographers
Political donors hot to trot
Marketeers chasing the money-shot
Death-threats from an anonymous bot
Live-streaming who's been shot and who's not
Via a search engine in the cloud
Tracking your every move on CCTV
Down to the sickle cells in our DNA
With all the Entry signs along the way
Saying Hate not Hope Hate not Hope Hate not Hope

Hooked on the rhythm
Fucked by the rhythm
Cross the blood-brain barrier at the wrong end of the prism

'If you haven't done anything wrong
Why fear what we harvest about you?
What biometric data, facial features
Medical records, political affiliations
Sexual orientation, private assignations
History of all you're buying
Could ever sell you down the Amazon without even trying'
Says Alexa , her voice the servant not the serpent.
This Deliveroo drone's no pie in the sky

This is how we got from Milton's Areopogitica
To Cambridge Analytica
To Faust's Mephistopheles
Handing over the golden keys,
To Blake's mind-forged manacles
Shackling our wrists and ankles,
Hostage to the rhythm
Clones of the rhythm
Zombies of the rhythm

Fancy algorithm　　　　　　*(to the tune of Gershwin's 'Fascinatin' Rhythm')*
You've got me on the go
Faster algorithm, I'm all a-quiver
What a fuss you're making
My mind just wants to know
Why I'm always shaking just like a fliver
Each morning I get up with the sun
- Start the-tapping, brain a-zapping-
Ten thousand steps and then my day's done -

The right brain is inclusive
Possesses the wisdom of the planet's kingdom
Works in tandem with the left brain
But drinks from a deeper spring of wonder
The vast vast waters of the petrel and the porpoise

Graeme Ryan

The Lunar Thorn

When the moon is a pale musk-rose in the sky
beware the lunar thorn

when the leather head-rest in your Lagonda emits a sigh
beware the lunar thorn

when Betelgeuse starts its knife-throwing turn
                              and Sirius feels the adrenaline burn
and Orion's cheeks (a la Dizzy Gillespie) bulge on his horn

beware the lunar thorn

big as the Horn of Africa is
                    it's no match for the scorpion sting, that lunar thing
of the thorn

O lunar thorn a drop of your dew, a tincture of you
is like Manuka honey -

but a lunar thorn's tip
is the shriek from a spark,
a cry from a quark,
a lunar thorn's liquor's best stored in the dark,
like money.

Tonight the moon is full and it's tempting -
but don't even dream of attempting -

you wouldn't go out would you?

Prick your thumbs
a cortege comes

opening coffin-deeps
and endless sleep.

Graeme Ryan

Fork and Spoon

At the Whitney she stands in front of Jasper John's *In Memory of My Feeling*, an homage to his break-up with Robert Rauschenberg.

A large charcoal gray canvas, two squares connected with traditional bronze hinges, creating a gentle seam down the middle of the large rectangle.

Enveloped in canvas darkness, she sees the dangling fork and spoon tied at the neck, hung by a thin cord looped like a noose from a nail at the painting's top.

The lovers hang entwined in perpetuity.

Barbara Sapienza

Heart In Hand

A woman, as old as the sun, sits on a bench holding a four-inch heart
ready to give it away or have it snatched and gobbled.

Perhaps she dreams a carnivore will eat her alive; or a soft vulnerable
human will sit beside her, take her hand, leave her heart intact.

Eyes closed, a serene grin, she sits outside day and night in all weathers.
Foggy mist bites her. Chilly, she cuddles into herself, her hand holding
the curved thing.

People pass, unsure whether to tell her to put her heart in her purse or
near to her generous bosom to keep it warm.

A family stops. The little girl says, "Mommy, look! A valentine in her
hand."
"Shh! she's sleeping," Mom says.
"Look, she's blinking," The girl pulls closer.

"This is too weird. Let's go." Mom pulls her away. When they stop at
the crosswalk the girl pushes away, sprints back, holds her red bonnet
from the wind, and stops in front of the dreaming woman.

"Why do you have a heart in your hand?" The girl points to the four-
inch heart.
"Don't touch it," says a man rushing in beside her. "You'll disappear."
His red spaghetti hair ruffles against soiled clothes. No shoes. "Bu shit.
Bu shit," he says. Eyes dull, humorless.

"Go away," the woman shouts to the man.
"Take this heart, and give it to your mom." She hands it to the girl.

"Mom doesn't need this." She faces the homeless man. "I'm giving this
to you." She leaves but not before seeing his eyes glisten.

Barbara Sapienza

Tony Spumoni

In 1950 Mama said that Mrs. Lucy D., my friend Ray's mother, spoke in broken English.

"Watch-a your mouth-a," she said to her kids when they sassed back; she put *a* or *o* at the end of every word; she was born in Italy; came here as a young woman. She wore tight curls, died her hair very black. She liked perms too. She and her husband were Mama and Daddy's friends. Her youngest, Ray-ray, was mine. He was five now. We played Doctor in the corner of my porch. We examined each other when he came over.

He usually came to my house except for the day Mama let me go over to his house to play. She watched us cross the street until I turned to wave goodbye, then Mama turned to go inside. I felt like a big girl. I followed Ray-ray up the stairs to his porch where we entered a small vestibule and walked a flight of narrow stairs to the second floor. The passageway was dark and narrow like a tunnel. I counted more than twenty steps almost the most I ever counted - as far as I could count as an almost five-year-old. There may have been more steps. I don't know.

We stopped at a landing in front of a closed door where I could hear something that sounded alive, making my insides wiggle.

"That's my sister Ro-Ro, she has to play piano everyday," he said, matter-of- factly. "This is my house, we practice every day."

I wasn't exactly sure what he meant. I didn't know if I had to practice anything at my house. We passed the closed door where the pretty music flowed through the cracks, filling the stairwell. At the second door Ray turned the knob into the small kitchen where the smell of chocolate made my mouth became wet.

"Come in, *venga*, close-a the *porta*," Mrs. Lucy D. said, using this strange language, one word English and one word Italian. Ray closed the door. Now the sound of the piano in the next room was louder. I wanted to dance.

"No disturb-a." Lucy closed the door from off the kitchen but not before I peaked in and saw the tall sister, sitting straight up with long fingers, curved gracefully playing a song and singing too.

"Si-tta," Mrs. Lucy said, handing us a spoon and a chocolate pudding. "*Prende* take-a." She placed the cup in front of my nose.

"*Mangia*, eat-a," she said.

I took the small spoon and dipped it into the creamy cup of pudding. My nose was pulled by the smell and dove into the chocolate before my spoon launched into what was the smoothest and creamiest texture I ever held in my mouth. My tongue exploded and water dripped out. I stared at the shiny dark mess of pudding, putting my spoon in and out - another and another spoon, each one better than the one before, going in until the cup was empty. I licked the insides of the glass bowl, licked my lips too.

Ray was playing with his pudding, turning his spoon round and round, building a point and then licking the peak like he was eating a chocolate ice cream cone.

Schiffo his mother said, pulling the cup away. I knew that word because my grandmother used it. It meant disgusting. But he pulled the cup back toward him, licking anyway. I envied him and wanted to lick the peak off his pudding. I couldn't understand how he was going so slowly. I took a look at the stovetop where at least a dozen more cups sat like handsome musicians, trumpeting a sweet aroma.

"May I have another?" I asked.

"No, *basta*. Enough-a," she said.

But my hand, as if it had a mind of its own, shot out, reaching for another one. "Can I have another one Mrs. Lucy? Please?" I asked, as my hand felt the warm glass.

"No," she said, "*basta*. Go play now."

I tasted salty tears, mixing with other tastes, sweet and bitter, making a weird concoction. I didn't want to show Mrs. Lucy what I felt. With so many cups on the stove, why couldn't I have one more? Was she mean? Stingy? Was I angry?

Ray filled his mouth with a big scoop, swallowed fast. "Let's go play," he said. He got up and I followed him to his room. I held my head down feeling something new, a feeling I didn't understand. I couldn't even see his trucks. They were all blurred. I looked at his closet and wished I could go inside and hide, think, maybe even cry; I didn't want to show Ray my tears. I was a big girl, almost five, in kindergarten.

"My mom's like that," he said, handing me his favorite ice cream truck, like the one that stopped on our corner, the one we waited for on summer days, the one we called Tony Spumoni like the song. That made me smile, but my head hurt and I couldn't wait to go home where Mama would let me eat whatever I wanted.

What was I to see? I took home a crack in my little shell like the crack in Humpty Dumpty. Something like shards of chocolate melted in my mind.

Was it about practice? Limits? Going slowly to savor? Pleasure? A wake-up call?

A recognition like a Zen temple bell, a Zen slap, startled me. What I would learn later to be a wake-up call, a call to change.

Ray had said there were times when he and his sister had to practice piano and song. There were times for one pudding. There were times for practice. There were times for *Tony Spumoni, the Ice Cream Man.*

Barbara Sapienza

Letting herself in

The curtains stay shut, blocking
the blackbirds' cheerful coupling.
The quiet clock faces the wall.
There is shame in the envy of birds.

She buys new shoes with silent soles,
a dress with side zips, cheaper underwear.
Black pens mark the disappointment
of frequent cancellations.

The hotel charges extra for a smaller room,
its digital singleness pushing dreams into walls.
There is no one here to remind her
to switch the light out.

She returns to find the house did not wait up,
its dark windows outnumber her
reflecting back an unfamiliar face
as she let herself in.

Helen Scadding

Pheasant at Taunton Station

She flew low over the roof of Platform Two,
clipped by the edge of a First Great Western.

Face down among the plastic bags
her tweed feathers fan out - a jaunty headdress.

Her reptilian feet point backwards,
exhibited, framed by silver track.

We stand holding polystyrene cups,
waiting obediently behind the yellow line

drawn to the blood of impact,
staring, as though at embers.

Helen Scadding

A Cup of Tea
(Mary Cassatt 1880)

First of all, the cup, of course.
Centred, white bone china, wedding-ringed,
the kind a clumsy aunt will drop and wreck the set.

A blue chair, as comforting as morphine,
waiting for its chance to become shabby chic.

Behind, a tub shaped like a baby's coffin
where a jungle of blooms jostle for attention,
one already on the turn.

Her arm, encased in a long, ivory glove
like a plaster cast, throbs and aches
but putting it down will spoil her sister's painting.

Her dress, tangerine with slashes
of anaemic pink, like a patient's gown
after a botched operation.

That slight swelling of her stomach
is not a sign that she is with child
or has over-indulged on fondant dainties.
Rather it hints at the medical something
with the unpronounceable name
that will shortly kill her.

So she gazes out, not at
guests with their fluting chit-chat
but at something else entirely.
She has already gone from here.

Yet when for the very first time
she looks at her portrait,
completed, finished, done,
she has never, ever felt more alive.

Dave Smith

Pushing up the Snowdrops
(i. m. Glyn Smith)

In Russia they call
corpses emerging from deep-freeze
as the winter snow slowly melts away snowdrops.
The drunkard for whom one for the road
was an easy mistake to make.
The wife whose Christmas present
was one punch too many.
But this is not Russia.

Once I knew a galanthophile.
Whose only fetish was
a passion for snowdrops.

All of those dainty drop-pearls
looked the same to me
but he was a sharp-eyed teacher
faced with a fresh September class
or a farmer naming each and every cow.
He knew his snowdrops.

He'd drool over bulb catalogues
at Galanthus Green Tear
or sigh with unrequited love
at Galanthus Elizabeth Howard, the only other woman
he was ever tempted by.

Once he speculated heavily
on Galanthus Ikariae, which staying hidden,
covered up like the perfect crime,
broke his heart, big as it was.

Far too early it was his turn to be covered up,
his coffin splashing into a waterlogged hole
as if we were burying him at sea.
No chance of him reappearing.

Instead, seeing these optimistic flowers
peeking through, I like to think
he's giving the first ones
a gentle push, encouraging
them to suss out the place before
that heave, spilling out the rest,
spreading like a juicy rumour.

"They'll clump up, given time," he'd told me
and as usual he's been exactly right.

Dave Smith

Malaya '59

The one thing I remember

about cutting kale was the

icy shards

that shuddered down

my ten year old neck

 when I grasped the gnarled stalk

slashed down with

the panga

also thinking about him

the sweat of fear

on his neck and

needing eyes

in the back of his head

fighting through

the bamboo.

David Smith

Melindy's Brother

Wild Bill's second wife has a bullet hole in her leg. She said it was her brother who shot her. I saw it when Melinda put one leg across her knee, a star shaped scar about the size of a dime. She wore cut-off jeans and her legs were brown against the lawn grass.

We were sitting around the picnic table as Bill and Leon fussed around with the outboard on the pontoon boat. All of us - Bill, Leon, Deena, Melinda and me were planning to go out for a day of putting around the lake. Some swimming, maybe. Drinking beer for sure.

Melinda was as tall as Bill, a Texas gal he met when he was still in the Air Force. Story is that Melinda went to the Enlisted Men's housing near the base and knocked on a door. Bill's wife, Bonnie, answered it and Melinda said to her, "Is Bill here?"

"No," Bonnie said. "He ain't. I'm Bill's wife. Who are you?"

"I'm Melindy. Bill sorta mentioned you once. I figured there's be more to you, I reckon." Bonnie was a one of the Jackson's from over near Gilman. All the Jackson's are on the short side and Bonnie barely cleared five feet. She and Bill had married when he was home after the second year in the service. Like all the Jackson's she was proud, too, and left Bill that very day to move back home.

He stayed in Texas. Shoot, I was maybe eight when he graduated from high school. When I was old enough me and Leon drove down to visit him. It had been in winter and we finally left snow behind when we crossed into Oklahoma. Leon was driving his Plymouth Fury and slowed when we hit the line.

"What you doing?" I asked. I liked the way the country went by at ninety miles an hour.

"Okie cops are notorious," he said. "Nobody speeds through here. Especially speeders who look us."

Leon had been driving for Foxtail Line and had drove a big rig all over. At times he had stopped and saw Leon while on the job.

"Look, Ray," he had said. "When you get back home don't tell the folks about what you see. No need to get the Old Man worked up."

He meant the dope. Bill had a dozen plants in a greenhouse and a few more in a root cellar behind the farmhouse he was renting. That part of Texas is cotton fields so the greenhouse windows were waxed over. From a distance the cotton bolls looked like snow. Bill met us at his house door with a Budweiser in his hand. He hugged Leon and slugged me on the shoulder.

"Sheeit," he said. "Look at little brother. You want a beer?"

"Bill," Leon said, "it's what, ten in the morning?"

Bill laughed. "For sure. Maybe we can crack an egg in it and make breakfast." He led us inside. Leon had met Melinda but no one else in the family had. We'd heard about her and seen Bonnie give us the stink eye once or twice. Heard Bill and Melinda had a daughter and the little thing ran up to her daddy. Bill swept Angela up and twirled her around. She was a cute as a button.

If I was the second of our family to meet Melinda it wasn't any big thing. She was wearing a Cowboys t-shirt and no bra, bell bottom jeans. She took Angela from Bill and nodded to me and Leon. "This one looks you," she said. I remember seeing a smudge of dirt on her bare toes.

"He does," Bill said. "Lucky man." Since leaving the Air Force Bill had got wooly.

"He is house broken," Leon said. "Barely. Sometimes he doesn't spill food on himself."

"Hey," I said. "I'm right here." Right away my brothers fall into old ways, picking on the youngest. "Bill," I said, "we brought you some stuff from home. Potatoes. Jars of canned goods and tomatoes."

"Sheeit," he said. "Bring it in. I'll fix us some breakfast. Mi casa, su casa," he said.

Bill had been a cook in the Air Force. He said that the best part was riding a big jet and making fancy food for the generals. Once he served the Secretary of Defense. In no time he had fixed us a pan of fried potatoes with onion and a skillet of thick bacon. Melinda carried a loaf of Wonder bread to us as we sat on the porch and ate. She then carried a pot of coffee out before sitting with us.

Without asking she poured Leon a cup. "You want some?" she asked me.

In the slight chill her nipples were poking into the t-shirt and I was afraid she saw me looking. "Nope," I said. "Thanks." Angela crawled up on her lap and Melinda gave her bits of potato. I could see Bill in her eyebrows and nose. I wished we'd have thought to bring a camera. Ma would be asking, I had thought.

But Ma had died of stroke before meeting Melinda and Dad not long after. Cancer. As we sat at the picnic table so many years later I thought about my parents. Family.

"Did it hurt?" I asked. "When you got shot?" I pointed at her leg.

"Nah. It was a .22. He was fooling around and it went off." She tapped a Kool from a pack and lit it. She waved toward the pontoon boat. "We going to go for a ride?"

"Oh sure. It's Leon's boat. It usually runs pretty good." Part of me was hoping it would take a little more to get it started. My Debbie would be getting off her shift at the clinic in an hour and maybe she could join us. Debbie likes to get out on the lake more than anybody. When I first met her she had swam ashore to emerge from the water at the Big Minnow. I was cutting the grass there and she walked right across it.

"You okay?" I had asked. The only boat around was distant and still going away.

"Tell you what," she said, "I rode the length of the lake on a dare but I ain't going to ride it back."

"You waterskied?"

"Course I did. Dad and his buddies drove and they tried to get me off. Making crazy turns into the wake. Now they owe me a hundred dollars." She was a year behind me in school and I had never noticed her before. That August day she wore a canary yellow bikini that glowed against her skin. I really wish she was coming with us today.

"Ray," Melinda said.

"Oh, what?"

"I asked if the water was going to be cold. Out there."

"Sure," I said. "If you dive down. It's always cold down deep. On top it will be nice."

She shook her head. "I don't know how y'all live up here. Even in summer it's cold."

"No chiggers," I said.

"Don't you start. I about got carried off last night by mosquitoes. And what was those things on Angela's legs? When she was swimming?"

"Leeches."

Melinda shuddered. "Nasty. No wonder Bill left."

"Uh-huh." Angela was fifteen now, the age I was when I met Melinda. I think of that when I see the lines around Melinda's eyes. She still wears tight shirts and I have to be careful where I let my eyes linger.

"Where is he at?" I asked. "Your brother. One who shot you."

"Roger? He went to Baton Rouge."

"He your only brother?"

"No, I got three. Roger is my favorite. Like you."

"What?"

"Like you are Bill's favorite brother."

"No way." I nodded toward where Leon and Bill stood over the outboard motor. "Leon and him are close."

"Maybe. But you're his favorite." She drew deep in the cigarette and I watched how she filled her chest. Frowned and let the smoke out her nose. "Before you came that time, to visit, all he talked about was you. Wait until you meet Ray-Ray. He's the genius. He blew away all those school tests."

"I was a weird kid."

"Nah. You just always had your nose in a book. Even when you visited Bill and me. Leon would be out on Bill's dirt bike or working on his car. We wouldn't know where you were and found you in the greenhouse with a book."

"You could get high in that greenhouse. From the transpiration."

She laughed. "Transpiration? What kinda word is that?"

"Vapor. The vapor from those marijuana plants."

"See what I mean? You weren't a weird kid. Just smarter than anybody else around."

I caught her eye. "You were something, too. I thought you were beautiful."

Melinda tipped her head back and laughed the way some women did. A delicious, throaty laugh that made Bill and Leon look our way. "Oh, hon," she said. "I knew that. You were always staring at me."

"Sorry." I heard the outboard motor cough to life.

She ground the cigarette into the tabletop. "Nah. Don't be. I knew it and it didn't bother me." She stood. "How cold did you say that water is?"

"Not cold at all."

"Just like your brother Bill," she said. "A smile and a lie. A smile and another lie."

Travis Stephens

Joyce Carol wants to go to the Library

Well? Where are you going? Oh? To "the library"? Is that so? Because I talked to my friend, Miss Marian the other night, and she said she didn't see you there at all.

You were in the music section? listening to records? Well, I don't believe it. They don't have any of your kind of music there.

A special grant? Well I never. Libraries are supposed to be stocked with good music. Classic music. Mozart. Brahms. Benny Goodman. Not your goofy Bob Dylan stuff.

A prophet, you say? A prophet of what? I'd say he's the prophet of the degradation of your generation. Don't talk to me about losing innocence, Joyce Carol, the fact that you're growing up is scary enough as is.

Let me tell you a story.

Let me tell you how young women lose their innocence.

Once upon a time . . . what? You used to love stories that started that way.

Once upon a time there was a country princess maiden who lived near the woods, and her mother told her not to go into the woods but she couldn't help it because there were cute little chipmunks and she would get together with her friends and they would play little charming spells with apple stems to see who their husbands would be. They thought it was just harmless white magic.

But then the day came that the country princess maiden's parents were out at the market and she was alone, stirring a pot of stew, when the devil came to her door and told her to come with him. She didn't want to but she didn't have a choice, because the devil had her apple stem, the one tied into the shape of a goat.

You don't believe me? I guess you're a little too old now for fairy tales. I heard this other story though, this one you should really pay attention too.

Just a few years ago, there was this man who lived in Tuscan. Not really a man, per se, more of a man-child. Never finished school. All he ever did was throw parties for his friends. Wild, unchaperoned parties where all sorts of unmentionable things occurred. When he was twenty-two, he decided that he liked one of his girlfriend's buddies. So he got all the information he could about this girl, where she lived, what she liked to do, and he found out that she liked to sneak out sometimes. She was just a young thing though! Only fifteen! He and his girlfriend drove over to her house and they convinced her to come with them, and then he drove her out into the desert and killed her.

Oh and that's not all. He did it to other girls too. I read all about it in Life. And he was so weird Joyce, I mean really strange. He'd wear make-up and stuff his boots so he'd look taller, probably looked like he had hooves for feet or something.

Oh, You've changed your mind about the Library? Now you want to borrow the typewriter instead? Just don't write anything too scary. All these stories are giving me goosebumps.

Megan Marie Sullivan

Crossing the border

I watch her fingers pull the needle
draw thread through open weave
silk strands slip through crotchety hands
as she counts spaces   left and right
fills gaps with fragments of her life.

Age-worn eyes scrape the fabric
for missed memories
do you remember, she asks, those
heat-hazed days of curlews' cries
when we walked on scrubby moorland

gazed at the far horizon.
Now no light can brighten eyes
that barely see   a lifetime in a frame
a border cross-stitched   wrapped
in tissue   waiting.

Kate Swann

Homecoming

After suit and briefcase
were put away for the day
he would stand
looking to the skies
Gauloise firmly clamped
between his lips
stopwatch in hand
direction and strength
of the wind
measured again.

I hadn't realised
how fickle air could be
how critical its behaviour
in the progress
of the 'favourite'
he taught me
what to look for in a champion.

When he caught sight
of a speck in the distance
he would start to whistle
high and slow
to guide a tired bird home
to be clocked
weighed   fed rich corn
him in his
dark grey overall
welcomed
a pale grey pigeon.

Kate Swann

Room 101

I am ripped from mummy's milky arms
as I dozed, puffed cheek on breast.
I am taken to Room 101
where fish swim across the walls,
sailboats tack in circles overhead,
deep sea divers chase whales,
chase dolphins, chase deep sea divers
an endless pursuit shutting out the light.
I am stripped, left to shiver
laid out on plastic, exposed
to the watery cold of this cell,
skin damp from cloth rubbed
over my bottom and privates,
subjected to prods and pokes,
pushes and pulls at my arms and legs.
My screams go unheard;
mummy must not hear me
through the walls of my dungeon.
I dare to peer up with a single eye.
It's him again.

David Thompson

The Delivery Room

It was like the Somme, I quipped
to a friend, yet really that was apt:
a stretcher bearer freshly volunteered
ready to give aid, not join battle,
proud to serve, excited by adventure,
full of nervous anticipation heading to the front;
then the firing starts
and I want to cower in the trench
but the screams and flow of blood
are a whistle to follow over the top,
eyes blinded by smoke, panicked cries of, Gas!
and what can I really do
with these thin bandages, scraps of gauze
and a water bottle held trembling to your lips?

David Thompson

Keepsakes

She focused on his lips as he spoke
Trying hard to read between the line
Knowing that he'd hide behind a joke
Hoping that, for once, he'd speak his mind
Fearing that he lied with every kiss
Proving that his heart was insincere
Wondering if her love was worth the risk
Reckoning the cracks would soon appear.

She'll focus on his lips as he speaks.
Somehow she can't see it in his eyes.
Feel it when his fingers touch her cheek.
Hear it every time he says goodbye.
She focuses on words locked in his head.
Sometimes a secret's better left unsaid.

Simon Tindale

and all I wanted to say to my parents was

did you know

autumn bled
through your bedroom walls
like poppies cut down in corn

how I listened

muted
by the dying fields
beyond my door

at thirteen

I was never meant
to hear
the last leaves

shivering in your polar wind

all I wanted
was apple blossom
in November

Julia Usman

Lament to a great aunt

After the coffin
the burial
I clear your house
and in the back of a cupboard
a mahogany box
with silver plaque

the engraved name
is youthful
giddy with italics
marking 21
a stranger
impersonating you.

I open the lid
reflect on the years
this canteen has waited
for a celebration, a christening
a memorable occasion
to un-tarnish the contents
that lie in their neat velvet bed

every spoon, knife, fork
so carefully placed
denied all purpose

the bone of their handles
as fine as your wrists

the years of anticipation
on your mother's advice
for that special day

the slow slow tarnish
of her words.

Julia Usman

October

a double-wide on a truck stirs
dry leaves on the road

the swamp behind my house is for sale
the government calls it a wetland

the old pony is set
to be put down Thursday

my son and I made a collage
of their younger selves to hang on a nail in the barn

we don't know his birthday
my son made it Wednesday

I don't invite him to watch
in case he doesn't go down easy

every time I close my eyes
I see the needle

my son won't see the backhoe dig
a pit behind the manure pile

the tines of the skid steer
maneuver under yellow coat

by the time the bus comes brittle leaves
will cover fresh dirt

Lyndsey Kelly Weiner

Spring Peepers

Called *crucifer* for the cross on their backs -
nights when the maple sap slows, their blood
cools to negative eight degrees.

At their first calls, the brown calf is born,
then the yellow, then my son -
his sandpaper mouth at my breast.

Cowbirds slip their eggs in foreign nests. The hollow click
of crayfish claws, a peeper's four pliable toes -
a slow-motion race up the screen door.

Peeping at 90 decibels - their lovers lay
a thousand eggs. My boy's father's last night
under the buzzing metal roof: only the males sing.

Lyndsey Kelly Weiner

Her Essence

resting her arthritic bones
like an old ghost
in a dreary municipal cemetery
and vexed over the fate of her cottage
now a home to strangers
who have left no vestige of the ninety years
she spent in this cradle of her being

after the sale
a whirlwind of refurbishments
paint to plumping,
kitchens to carpets,
doors to down pipes ....
.....Victorian to Post Modern Contemporary
and the odour of fresh flat Farrow & Ball

then one Easter Eve
an invitation to visit
from the next set of new owners
"What has changed since
the old lady's death?"
"Everything, down to the screws in the floorboards"

but climbing the stairs
there was suddenly the essence
of her old furniture polish
(a mixture of beeswax and lavender)
the fragrance of woodsmoke
(from a bricked-up fireplace)
and the aroma of her Welsh cakes
(fresh from the long-scrapped Triplex Stove Cooker)

"Yes, we have felt a presence here"

Owen Williams

The Veteran

Waking from a nightmare dream of desert storms, the cut of cold air
slices through the forlorn abandoned door well of his observation post.

This is neither Kandahar nor Helmand province but his wounded mind
endures there and the bullets of iced hail cowers his fragile mettle.

A kind coffee from a dark stranger confuses his wary perception
and then unexpected coins drop like mortars in his threadbare army beret.

All day long he stares blankly at the passing traffic with hardtack rations,
always scanning up and down the shabby street for hidden IEDs.

Confused, he backs against the door's cold glass, as every passer by
conceals a suicidal vest and eager now to please his god with martyrdom.

Night falls and time to hunker down, for the enemy unseen may ambush his
sanity at any moment; there is no advance or retreat from this battle.

Owen Williams

About the Contributors

Lizzie Ballagher's work has appeared in magazines and webzines on either side of the Atlantic.
Find her blog at https://lizzieballagherpoetry.wordpress.com/

Clare Bercot Zwerling is a newer poet. Her work appears in numerous journals and publications. She resides on the Mendocino Coast of California.

Margaret Beston is widely published, the author of two collections - *Long Reach River* (2014) and *Timepiece* (2019), and a pamphlet *When the Ground Crashed Upwards*, 2020 - also the founder of Roundel in Tonbridge.

Zanna Beswick's poetry has been published in *The Independent*, *The International Times*, *The French Literary Review*, *Resurgence* etc., in several anthologies, and read on R4's 'Poetry Please'.

Christina Buckton lives near Cambridge. So far she has three Guernsey awards and has poems published in *The North*, *Orbis* and *Stand*. Her collection, *Holding it Together*, is published by Lamplight Press in April 2022.

James Callan grew up in Minneapolis, and now lives in New Zealand, with his wife, Rachel, and his son, Finn. His work has appeared or is forthcoming in *Bridge Eight*, *Beyond Queer Words*, *The Tiny Journal*, and *The Plentitudes Journal*.

Ray Clark is author of the highly acclaimed IMP series: gritty, crime fiction novels featuring detectives Gardener and Reilly, set in the West Yorkshire city of Leeds.

Nigel Ferrier Collins is a writer and visual artist whose poems have appeared in magazines including *Poetry Review*. In a career in education he contributed to journals and had books published by OUP and Heinemann.

Adele Cordner's pamphlet *The Kitchen Sink Chronicles* was published by Hedgehog Poetry Press in 2021 and her new collection *Tea & Toast* will be published in 2022. Her poems have been placed in numerous competitions.

Charlotte Cosgrove is a writer and lecturer from Liverpool, England. Her first book of poetry *Silent Violence with Petals* will be published later this year. Charlotte is the editor for Rough Diamond poetry journal.

R C de Winter writes in several genres with a focus on poetry, which appears in several top literary journals. Her work is also included in many anthologies.

Phil Dunkerley lives in South Lincolnshire, where he takes part in a range of poetry groups and open mic events. His poems have appeared in a fair number of journals, webzine and anthologies. He reviews for *Orbis*.

Marie-Rose Goto-Švić is an emerging writer from Australia, living in Japan. Her crime fiction novel *The Kids Aren't Alright* was selected as a finalist for the 2021 Page Turner Writing Award.

A novelist and poet, Ian Gouge is the creator of **Coverstory** *books* and the driving force behind *New Contexts*. His latest works include *On Parliament Hill* (a novel) and *The Homelessness of a Child* (poetry).

Kris Green lives in Florida with his wife, two-year-old son, a new baby daughter. Last year, he had three short stories published. As of March of this year, he's had 6 stories and 2 poems published.

Lucy Heuschen is a London-born poet living in Germany. She is the founder of The Rainbow Poems online community. Her pamphlet *We Wear The Crown* will be published by Hedgehog Press in Summer 2022.

Diana Killi is a retired language teacher and translator, currently living in York. She has been writing poetry since retirement and has built up a collection of poems. This is her first try at publication.

Richard Knott's books include *The Sketchbook War*, *The Trio* and *The Secret War Against the Arts*. His poetry collection *Perfect Day* was published in 2020. His poems have appeared in *Selcouth Station, The Cannon's Mouth* and *Line Breaks*.

Richard Lester draws you into stories of people and places. His work is carved in the Radius sculpture, published in international magazines and is *a celebration of ordinary magic perceived by a keen eye.*

Lindy Newns is a poet and playwright from Manchester. Her poems have appeared in various journals and anthologies, including the *Poems for Grenfell* anthology. She was shortlisted for a Northern Writers' Poetry Award in 2021.

Dante Novario is a writer from Louisville, KY. Nominated for both the 2020 pushcart and rhysling awards, his writing has appeared in numerous journals, magazines and podcasts.

Alfie Ormsbee is a transgender poet and educator from Michigan. He has been published in numerous anthologies, including *The Heart of Pride*, *New Contexts: 2, High Shelf Press*, and *Aurora*.

Carol Park reads, teaches, gardens, hikes and writes of California and Japan. Both have shaped her. She studied writing with Seattle Pacific University. Her novel, forthcoming, is set in 1990's Tokyo. Find her at <u>CarolPark.us</u>.

Janet Philo is published online and in print. Her two pamphlets include *Cheap Fish for Kings* (Black Light Engine Room, 2020). She also has work in *The Best New British and Irish Poets 2019-2021* (The Black Spring Press Group)

Jenna Plewes's latest collections *A Woven Rope* (V.Press) and *The Salt and Sweet of Memory* (Dempsey and Windle) are both being sold by her in aid of Freedom from Torture. Find her on Poetry PF or on Facebook.

Stephen Poole is a retired policeman. His poems have appeared in *The Ekphrastic Review, Poetry on the Lake,* and *LPP Magazine. New Contexts: 3* is the third anthology to publish his work.

David Punter lives and works in Bristol, and has published eight poetry collections, the latest of which are *Those Other Fields* (Palewell, 2020) and *Stranger* (Cinnamon, 2021).

Jenny Robb has written poetry since retiring. From 2020 – 2022 she's been published in online and print magazines and anthologies. Her debut collection, The Doll's House, will soon be published by Yaffle Press.

Graeme Ryan lives near Exmoor. His poetry is featured on *Bard Window* and in various competitions and publications. In March 2022 he published his debut poetry collection *Valley of the Kings* with Coverstory Books.

Barbara Sapienza lives in Sausalito and is a retired clinical psychologist. She has a novel being published in Spring 2023, *The Dream Being, A Novel,* to add to *Anchor Out,* 2017 and *The Laundress,* 2020.

Helen Scadding has had work published in *Artemis, South, Orbis, Reach Poetry* and several anthologies. She has a distinction in Creative Writing (MA Exeter) and is now working on her debut pamphlet.

Dave Smith, a retired English teacher, is certain that the perceptive fellow-poets in Derby Stanza have been vital in helping him to find his voice.

David Smith lives in North Yorkshire. His work has appeared in *The Sid Chaplain Short Story Anthology, Red Squirrel Press* and *Assent*. His latest book *Only Rumour Survives* was published by Coverstory books in 2021.

Travis Stephens is a tugboat captain who lives and works in California. His book of poetry, *"skeeter bit & still drunk",* is available at Finishing Line Press or on Amazon.

Megan Marie Sullivan graduated from Northwestern University with an MA in Creative Writing in 2012. Her work has previously appeared in *In Parenthesis,* and *OPEN: Journal of Arts and Literature.*

Kate Swann is a Northern, rural poet with an eye for detail. Family, friends and travel are important to her life and none escape her pen when she is writing.

David Thompson is a poet from Droitwich Spa, Worcestershire. His work has featured in magazines and anthologies such as *Atrium, Magma, Orbis* and *New Contexts: 1* (Coverstory Books, 2021).

Simon Tindale was born in Sunderland, wrote songs in South London and found poetry in West Yorkshire and is currently working on a first collection.

Julia Usman has had numerous articles and poems published in the UK and Australia. Her debut collection *She Who Sings Is Not Always Happy* was published by Coverstory Books (2021). She lives in Swaledale, North Yorkshire.

Lyndsey Kelly Weiner is a graduate of Stonecoast MFA and teaches writing at Syracuse University. She blogs at haikuveg.com.

Owen Williams, a graduate of Loughborough University and a teacher by profession, has always enjoyed reading poetry and has been writing seriously since 2016.

Recent publications from **Coverstory** *books*

Valley of the Kings by Graeme Ryan

Valley of the Kings is both excavation of family history and an incantation of voices telling contemporary stories that startle. The grieving son and the street angel; the coke addict meeting Piers Plowman in the service-station; the singing nightingale on Universal Credit; the homeless person in Ancient Egypt; the famous sax player; the young lovers in their mythic hotel: all united in 'the exquisite ache of the human day'.

Let 'the weight of the wind on tide' sing loud in this visionary debut which, in Graeme Ryan, introduces an exciting new voice to the UK poetry scene.

New Contexts: 2 - various authors

In many ways making the selection of pieces to include in *New Contexts: 2* was a much more difficult task than it had been for the inaugural edition of *New Contexts*. This was largely due to three factors.

The first was the breadth of submissions. For *New Contexts: 2* the geographical spread of contributors was much greater with many more offerings from the United States, and others from as far afield as Australia and New Zealand. Inevitably with such diversity comes a wider range of voices and styles - which led to some interesting dilemmas when trying to compare 'apples with pears'.

Secondly, the themes of the work offered for consideration were much more varied, including far fewer that were Covid-related. There were more submissions that touched on fundamental topics such as sexuality, diversity, and the political.

And thirdly, there were a greater proportion of prose submissions than for New Contexts: 1 - and a small number of pieces that seemed to have their feet rooted in both poetry and prose camps.

All of which made the final selection challenging.

Overall, I would like to believe that we have been able to strike an acceptable balance - prose versus poetry, the innovative versus the traditional - in terms of content, theme, and voice.

Making Marks in the Sand - various authors

The nature of relationships dominates this international collection of contemporary short stories; not just relationships between people, but also between individuals and their pasts and, in consequence, their potential futures.

The British and Continental American authors of *Making Marks in the Sand* explore the nature of love, regret and loss, peeling back the veneer on everyday life.

Often gritty, this is a powerful and moving collection.

Only Rumour Survives by David Smith

This eclectic collection sings with melancholy, humour, wistful reflection and evocative insight. Written in a concise style that makes for rare accessibility to inner meaning, this is a thought-provoking and original collection of poems. David Smith is also the author of *The Stencil Room*.

David Smith's poems are often concise and "interweave the varied and numerous antagonisms inherent in lived experience" - Bob Beagrie, Lecturer Teesside University.

Only Rumour Survives is David's fourth collection.

Shrapnel from a Writing Life by Ian Gouge

Shrapnel from a Writing Life is not a conventional book. It is neither fiction nor poetry, though it contains elements of both; nor is it strictly autobiographical, though it does present a partial life seen through a very particular lens. Also, it is not a book which lends itself to be 'read' in a standard manner; there is no 'normal' narrative flow to permit such an experience.

The majority of the text concerns itself with the notes made during thirty-seven years as the author attempted to work out not only what to write, but how to write; as he became absorbed in the minutiae of plot and character during the process of weighing-up or refining an idea. And it also lays bare the considerable angst which accompanies such struggle. Thus rough notes on an idea for a novel might be followed by more generic planning, consideration of the impact of paid work on his writing life, the nature of writing versus art, or the output from the kind of internal debates surely all writers must experience.

In its own way it is a remarkable endeavour - and a remarkably ambitious one. The tenacity of the author - in both keeping his notebooks alive for so many years, and then committing them to paper - requires equally tenacious readers; readers who can sift through these pages looking for nuggets as if they were panning for gold.